D0685295

GAY
MARRIAGE

Other Books in the At Issue Series:

GAY MARRIAGE

David Bender, *Publisher*
Bruno Leone, *Executive Editor*

Brenda Stalcup, *Managing Editor*
Scott Barbour, *Series Editor*

Tamara L. Roleff, *Book Editor*

An Opposing Viewpoints® Series

Greenhaven Press, Inc.
San Diego, California

Library of Congress Cataloging-in-Publication Data

Gay marriage / Tamara L. Roleff, book editor.
     p.   cm. — (At issue)
    Includes bibliographical references and index.
    ISBN 1-56510-693-8 (hardcover: alk. paper). —
ISBN 1-56510-692-X (pbk. : alk. paper)
    1. Gay couples—United States. 2. Gay marriage—United States.
3. Marriage law—United States. 4. Gay couples—Legal status, laws,
etc.—United States. 5. Gay marriage—Moral and ethical aspects—
United States. I. Roleff, Tamara L., 1959– . II. Series: At issue
(San Diego, Calif.)
HQ76.3.U5G387   1998
306.84'8—dc21   97-26614
                                                      CIP

Table of Contents

Introduction

For thousands of years, most cultures around the world have recognized marriage as a union between men and women. In the majority of modern nations, including the United States, same-sex couples cannot be legally married. Several gay couples unsuccessfully filed lawsuits in the latter half of the twentieth century against various states for not allowing them to marry. However, same-sex marriages were never considered possible in the United States until three same-sex couples challenged Hawaii's marriage law on the grounds that it discriminated against them based on their sex.

In response to the suit, Hawaiian health director John C. Lewin, who was responsible for issuing marriage licenses, filed a motion for dismissal. He argued that Hawaiian law recognizes marriage only as "a union between a man and a woman"; that the state's marriage laws do not "burden, penalize, infringe, or interfere in any way with the [plaintiffs'] private relationships"; and that the state is under no obligation "to take affirmative steps to provide homosexual unions with its official approval." The First Circuit Court agreed that the three couples did not have a valid complaint and dismissed the case.

Ninia Baehr and her coplaintiffs appealed the dismissal to the Hawaii Supreme Court, which, in a controversial 1993 decision, overturned the lower court's dismissal and remanded the case back to court for trial. The supreme court ruled that the state was required to prove the constitutionality of the Hawaiian Marriage Law and the state's compelling interest in restricting marriage to opposite-sex couples. The case, *Baehr v. Miike*, finally went to trial in September 1996, with Lewin replaced by the new health director, Lawrence H. Miike.

The Defense of Marriage Act

Also in September 1996, in anticipation of the Hawaii trial, Congress passed and Bill Clinton signed the Defense of Marriage Act (DOMA). The act defines marriage for federal purposes as "a legal union of one man and one woman as husband and wife," thus denying same-sex spouses any federal benefits that are automatically given to opposite-sex spouses. The act also gives states the option of not recognizing same-sex marriages performed in other states. Supporters of the Defense of Marriage Act were concerned that if same-sex marriage was declared legal in Hawaii, gays and lesbians would go to Hawaii to get married and then return to their home states. These states would then be forced to recognize such marriages under the Full Faith and Credit Clause of the U.S. Constitution, which requires states to recognize official acts, records, and judicial proceedings—such as marriages and divorces—performed in other states. The DOMA was designed to prevent this scenario by giving states permission to not recognize same-sex marriages performed in other states.

As DOMA was being debated in Congress, *Baehr v. Miike* went to trial. The state argued that same-sex marriages would threaten the health and welfare of children and families. The state also claimed that it had a compelling interest in promoting procreation within a marriage and in ensuring that Hawaiian marriages would be recognized in other states. Judge Kevin Chang found, however, that the state failed to prove its case, noting that even some of the state's witnesses admitted that same-sex couples could be good parents to their children. Therefore, he ruled, prohibiting same-sex couples from marrying discriminates on the basis of sex and is unconstitutional. Chang issued an order staying his verdict until the state's appeal could be heard before the Hawaii Supreme Court. Shortly afterward, the Hawaii state legislature approved a proposal that would amend the state constitution to ban same-sex marriages. The ballot initiative was expected to be voted on by Hawaiian residents in late 1998.

Gay marriage is immoral

Opponents of same-sex marriage contend that homosexuality is immoral and that allowing gay marriage would amount to society's condoning an immoral lifestyle. They maintain that legalizing same-sex marriage would force Americans to accept behavior of which the majority does not approve. Moreover, critics argue, marriage is by definition a union between a man and a woman; allowing a same-sex couple to marry degrades the institution of marriage and violates family values. According to Robert Knight, cultural studies director for the Family Research Council in Washington, D.C., marriage "is the building block of civilization. Equating a homosexual relationship with what Mom and Dad do devalues the whole concept of marriage."

More importantly, assert many DOMA supporters, the purpose of marriage is procreation; a same-sex couple is biologically unable to have children, thereby defeating the purpose of marriage. John Leo, a nationally syndicated columnist, writes, "Society has a crucial stake in protecting the connection between sex, procreation, and a commitment to raise children. If it didn't, why would the state be involved with marriage at all?"

Gay marriage is a right

Proponents of gay marriage argue, however, that society should support all kinds of committed relationships, heterosexual and homosexual. Author Bruce Bawer maintains that marriage "is an essentially conservative act to encourage couples, whether gay or straight, to settle down and take responsibility for each other." Furthermore, supporters contend that it is illogical and unfair to deny gay men and lesbians the right to marry because they cannot biologically have children together. They point out that many same-sex couples raise children conceived in earlier heterosexual relationships, some have adopted or foster children, and others have children conceived by artificial insemination. Besides, gay rights advocates assert, a parent's sexuality is no indication of his or her fitness as a parent; the primary quality of parenting, they contend, is the loving and nurturing relationship between parent and child.

Perhaps the most important point of all, gay marriage supporters insist, is that gays and lesbians should have the equal right to marry the one they love. Prohibiting them from marrying is discrimination, commentators contend, and denies them many benefits accorded to heterosexual couples who marry, such as the right of survivorship for homes, pensions, Social Security, and savings; joint tax returns; and joint insurance policies. Furthermore, they assert, granting gays and lesbians the right to marry and the inherent benefits that accompany that right will have little or no effect on heterosexual married couples. Representative Ed Fallon argued before the Iowa legislature, "Marriage licenses aren't distributed on a first-come first-served basis here in Iowa. Heterosexual couples don't have to rush out and claim marriage licenses now, before they are all snatched up by gay and lesbian couples." Gay marriage advocates reject the contention that same-sex marriage would pose a threat to the traditional family structure or to the mores of society.

The debate over gay marriage is especially controversial because it touches on the sensitive areas of family, sexual morality, and social justice. The diversity of views on this subject are reflected in *At Issue: Gay Marriage.* Although many of the selections included in this anthology were written prior to the passage of the Defense of Marriage Act and the decision in the *Baehr v. Miike* case, they present cogent arguments on the potential positive or negative effects of legalizing same-sex marriage.

1

Gay Marriage Should Be Legal

Andrew Sullivan

Andrew Sullivan, the former editor of the weekly magazine New Republic, *is the author of* Virtually Normal: An Argument About Homosexuality.

Gays and lesbians want to marry for the same reason as heterosexual couples—to demonstrate their love and commitment. The definition of marriage has changed over the centuries to recognize the human dignity of women and minorities; it should be changed again to recognize the dignity of gays and lesbians. Allowing gays and lesbians to marry would not lead to polygamy or bestiality, but would instead promote stability, responsibility, and family values.

Editor's note: Andrew Sullivan testified against the Defense of Marriage Act before the House Judiciary Committee's Subcommittee on the Constitution on May 15, 1996. The act, which was signed into law by Bill Clinton in September 1996, defines marriage as "a legal union between one man and one woman as husband and wife," and gives states the option of not recognizing same-sex marriages performed in other states.

L et me say first of all how honored I am to be here today. I immigrated to this country as a student twelve years ago and never dreamt I could be a part of this historic discussion. It says something particularly to me about this country's extraordinary capacity for inclusion and for freedom of speech that I can be here. I have come to love my adopted country and to believe in its promise—in its being a beacon to the world of the virtues of inclusion and equality, which are what, I believe, in part, we are discussing today.

You will hear this afternoon and in the coming days, many things about gay men and lesbians both in this country and around the world: that we are opposed to the traditional family, that we want to subvert America, that we are a powerful lobby that aims to destroy the sacred institution of marriage.

From Andrew Sullivan, testimony at the Hearing before the Subcommittee on the Constitution, House Committee on the Judiciary, 104th Cong., 2nd sess., on H.R. 3396, Defense of Marriage Act, May 15, 1996.

But that is not the truth of who we are.

We are your sons and daughters, your brothers and sisters, your aunts and uncles, in some cases even, your mothers and fathers. We are your co-workers and fellow members of Congress; your teachers and factory workers; your soldiers and nurses and priests. We are in every town and city in America; in every church and synagogue and mosque. We are in every American family—somewhere.

And like anybody else, we do not seek to destroy marriage; we seek to strengthen it.

We do not seek equality in marriage because we despise the institution of marriage—but because we believe in it and cherish it and want to support it.

People ask us why we want marriage, but the answer is obvious. It is the same reason that anyone would want marriage. After the crushes and passions of adolescence, some of us are lucky enough to meet the person we truly love. And we want to commit to that person in front of our family and country for the rest of our lives. It's the most natural, the most simple, the most human instinct in the world.

[Gays] do not seek to destroy marriage; we seek to strengthen it.

The real question, then, is surely not: why would gay men and lesbians want the right to marry?

It is: why on earth would anyone want to exclude us from it?

You will be told that, since the Torah, marriage has been between a man and a woman and that Western society has been built upon that institution. But we do not dispute that. Like you, we celebrate it. We were all born into the heart of the heterosexual family and we love our mothers and fathers. We seek to take away no one's right to marry; we only ask that those of us who are gay, through no choice of our own, be allowed the same opportunity.

You will be told that marriage is *by definition* between a man and a woman and that that is the end of the argument. But that cannot be the end of the argument. For centuries, marriage was *by definition* a contract where the wife was the legal property of her husband. And we changed that. For centuries, marriage was *by definition* between two people of the same race. And we changed that. We changed these things because we recognized that the human dignity of a person is the same whether that person is a man or a woman, black or white. We are arguing now that the human dignity of gay people is as profound as anyone else's and that marriage should begin at last to recognize that fact.

You will be told that marriage is only about the rearing of children. But we know that isn't true. We know that our society grants marriage licences to people who choose not to have children, or who, for some reason, are unable to have children. And that is as it should be. So the question is: why should two gay people who cannot have children be treated any differently?

You will be told that this is a slippery slope toward polygamy and other things—pedophilia or bestiality. But of course, same-sex marriage is the opposite of those things. The freedom to marry would mark the *end* of the slippery slope for gay men and lesbians, who right now have no institutions to guide our lives and loves, no social support for our relationships, no institution that can act as a harbor in the emotional storms of our lives.

As many conservative thinkers have noted, and I have argued in many places, this is an essentially conservative measure. It seeks to promote stability, responsibility, and the disciplines of family life among people who have been historically cast aside to the margins of our society. What could be a more conservative project than that? Why indeed would any conservative seek to oppose those very family values for gay people that he or she supports for everybody else?

These, of course, are arguments that we as a society have only begun to grapple with. They are matters of great importance that we need to debate carefully and seriously—around the kitchen table, in our homes and in the states where marriage has always been decided.

Which is why this bill is such a radical and unconservative measure.

Even if you disagree with me about the value of same-sex marriage, you should still oppose this bill. It is designed to shut down our public debate before it has even begun; it is intended to raise the issue in an election period where it is most difficult to treat these issues with the calm and depth they deserve; it is intended to divide Americans on an issue where we haven't even had a chance to have a full and measured discussion.

No rush

There is, after all, no rush. There are no same-sex marriages anywhere right now in the United States. The earliest any change could happen is toward the end of 1998, when the final appeal to the supreme court of the state of Hawaii is likely to be decided. Why do we have to force a decision now?

Let us take the next two years to let the people and the states decide for themselves.

If there is a question about the full faith and credit clause of the Constitution, let the Supreme Court decide, as it alone can, the constitutionality of the matter.

Let us not use this issue as a political football to score cheap points off people's lives and dignity. Let us instead treat each other with the respect we deserve, and debate this issue in calm and due time. I urge you to vote against this bill.

2

Prohibitions Against Same-Sex Marriage Are Unconstitutional

American Civil Liberties Union

The American Civil Liberties Union is a national organization that works to defend civil rights guaranteed by the U.S. Constitution.

The Defense of Marriage Act, which denies federal recognition of same-sex marriages and gives states the right to not recognize same-sex marriages performed in other states, is unconstitutional and unfair. The act discriminates on the basis of sex by making the ability to marry dependent on one's gender. The act also violates the Full Faith and Credit Clause of the Constitution, which requires that all states recognize the legal judgments of other states. Prohibiting gays and lesbians from marrying denies them the protection from discrimination that civil marriage provides.

Editor's note: The ACLU's statement supporting same-sex marriage was submitted as testimony to the Senate Committee on the Judiciary on July 10, 1996. The Defense of Marriage Act was signed into law by Bill Clinton in September 1996.

The American Civil Liberties Union believes that S. 1740, the Defense of Marriage Act, is unconstitutional, and that it is bad public policy.

The ACLU supports legal recognition of lesbian and gay relationships, and it believes lesbians and gay men should have the right to marry. Nothing else would accord complete legal equality to lesbians, gay men and bisexuals.

Civil marriage is the way our society defines one's most intimate, committed relationships; it is the only vehicle our society has for recognizing the existence of primary relationships not defined by blood. That has powerful emotional consequences, and powerful practical consequences as well. Our society uses marriage to identify our partners for everything from retirement programs, to critical medical decisions, to the simple right to be together in crisis situations, like hospital emergency rooms.

From the American Civil Liberties Union, testimony at the Hearing before the Senate Committee on the Judiciary, 104th Cong., 2nd sess., on S. 1740, a bill to define and protect the institution of marriage, July 11, 1996.

While S. 1740 does not itself deny lesbians and gay men the right to marry, it would for the first time deny federal recognition to state licensed marriages. Clearly, this legislation is designed to be a preemptive strike to nullify the rights that may be conferred by Hawaii and other states to same sex couples.

S. 1740 would also for the first time make it federal policy that a state is free to disregard some marriages of some couples who were legally married in another state. This could have very unfair, and in some cases tragic consequences for couples who travel across the country because their jobs are transferred to other states, or because of the desire to be near relatives, or for any number of legitimate reasons. Among the consequences of S. 1740 would be to deny federal recognition of a state sanctioned marriage and the rights to:

- take *bereavement or sick leave to* care for a partner or a partner's child;
- qualify for *pension or social security continuation* when a partner dies;
- keep a jointly owned home if a partner goes on *Medicaid;*
- file *joint tax returns* and quality for spousal exemptions on income and estate taxes;
- qualify for *veterans' discounts* on medical care, education and home loans based on a partner's service;
- apply for *immigration and residency* for partners from other countries.

We also believe that it is extremely unwise to proceed with this legislation without the benefit of additional hearings. This legislation raises complex legal questions that should be fully considered by Members of Congress before they are compelled to cast their vote.

Constitutional issues

S. 1740 is unconstitutional because it constitutes discrimination against lesbians and gay men under the due process clause of the Fifth Amendment and because it violates Article IV, Section 1 of the Constitution (the "Full Faith and Credit" Clause).

First, S. 1740 violates Article IV, Section 1 of the Constitution (the "Full Faith and Credit" Clause). Article IV says:

> Full faith and credit shall be given in each state to the public acts, records, and judicial proceedings of every other state. And the Congress may by general laws prescribe the manner in which such acts, records and proceedings shall be proved, and the effect thereof.

Section 2 of S. 1740 would allow state courts to ignore judgments from courts in other states "respecting" marriages between two persons of the same sex. Among the judgments which typically involve marriage are judgments of divorce, judgments awarding support or dividing property in connection with a divorce or separation, and judgments about obligations incurred because of marriage, like loan obligations, and obligations to vendors like hospitals, health care providers.

The United States Supreme Court has ruled again and again that the

Full Faith and Credit clause obligates every state to respect the judgments of other state courts, including judgments of divorce. See, e.g., *Williams v. North Carolina*, 317 U.S. 287, 294 (1947); *Sherrer v. Sherrer*, 334 U.S. 343, 354–356 (1948).

The court has allowed two limited exceptions to that rule. First, a forum state does not have to respect the judgment of a sister state that purports to transfer title to real estate within the forum state. Second, a state does not have to respect "penal" judgments from other state courts. See, e.g., *Fall v. Eastin*, 215 U.S. 1 (1909) and *Huntington v. Attrill*, 146 U.S. 657 (1892). Neither of those exceptions could remotely be stretched to fit S. 1740. Moreover, there is no "policy" exception. States which disagree with the policy behind a law on which a judgment is based must enforce the judgment nonetheless. See, e.g., *Williams v. North Carolina, supra,* 317 U.S. at 294, *Sherrer v. Sherrer, supra,* 334 U.S. at 354–356; and see *Fauntleroy v. Lum*, 210 U.S. 230, 237 (1908).

Civil marriage is the way our society defines one's most intimate, committed relationships.

While the Supreme Court has never decided what it means to say that one state must accord Full Faith and Credit to a state-created "status" like a marriage outside the context of a judgment, it seems clear that at a minimum, states are not free to completely ignore them. The Commerce Clause and the right to travel from state to state, even without Article IV, would seem to prevent states from ignoring marriages in interstate commercial transactions, or when the people of one state travel to another. See, e.g., *Shapiro v. Thompson*, 394 U.S. 618, 629 (1969).

Moreover, while Article IV doubtless gives Congress the power to decide how the judgments and acts of one state are to be proven in another, that power does not extend to nullifying Article IV's basic requirement of Full Faith and Credit. Congress can not, under the guise of deciding what effect to give to judgments and acts which have been proven under a mechanism it has created, decide that no Faith and Credit need be given at all. See, e.g., *Powell v. McCormack*, 395 U.S. 486, 550 (1969) (Congress has the power to decide if its members have the qualifications set out in the Constitution, but it may not, in the guise of doing so, manufacture additional qualifications). See also, *Thomas v. Washington Gas Light Co.,* 448 U.S. 261, 272 n. 18 (1980). That, however, is precisely what the bill purports to do.

Equal protection

Second, this entire bill violates the equal protection guarantee of the Due Process Clause of the Fifth Amendment. The third section of the bill creates a definition of marriage for all federal purposes. The definition says that a marriage means "only a legal union between one man and one woman." Just as the law struck down in *Loving v. Virginia*, 388 U.S. 1 (1967) discriminated on the basis of race because it made one's ability to marry depend on one's race, this bill discriminates on the basis of sex because it makes one's ability to marry depend on one's gender. It matters not that neither men nor women are unequally disadvantaged by the ban; whites and blacks were punished alike for violating the law in *Loving* as well. *Loving v. Virginia,* 388 U.S. at 11. The right to equality is a personal right, not a group right. See, *Regents of the University of California v. Bakke,* 438 U.S. 265, 289–290 (1978).

Classifications which discriminate on the basis of gender must be substantially related to some important government purpose. *Craig v. Boren,* 429 U.S. 190, 204 (1976). The only justification for the classification that appears from the proponents of the bill is that it would preserve what they regard as the "traditional" understanding of marriage. See Senator Don Nickles, "The Defense of Marriage Act." Quite apart from the fact that this ignores a 200-year tradition of allowing each state to define marriage, and using those definitions for federal purposes, tradition by itself is not an important government purpose. If it were, sex discrimination would be quite permissible; discrimination against women has a pedigree in tradition at least as long and time honored as that of discrimination against same-sex couples in marriage. See, e.g., *Bradwell v. State,* 83 U.S. 130, 141 (1873) (Bradley, J., concurring); and see *Stanton v. Stanton,* 421 U.S. 7, 14–15 (1975).

Furthermore, to the extent that S. 1740 was intended to disadvantage lesbians and gay men it is constitutionally suspect for that reason as well. This bill disenfranchises lesbians and gay men in their efforts to gain recognition for their most intimate relationship. In our view, sexual orientation classifications should be treated as suspect, like race and, we believe, gender classifications. See *Watkins v. U.S. Army,* 837 F.2d 1428, affd. on other grounds, 875 F.2d 699 (9th Cir. 1989); *contra High Tech Gays v. D.I.S.C.O.,* 895 F.2d 563 (9th Cir. 1990). But regardless of whether Courts treat classifications which disadvantage lesbians and gay men as suspect, it is clear that like all other classifications, they must serve some legitimate governmental purpose. A mere desire to harm the group which is disadvantaged is not a legitimate purpose. *United States Department of Agriculture v. Moreno,* 413 U.S. 528, 534 (1973); *Romer v. Evans,* ___ U.S. ___, 64 U.S.L.W. 4353, 4356–4357 (1996). Yet S. 1740 rests on nothing more. Saying that discrimination is nothing new and that one would like to keep it up does not come close to explaining what legitimate interest a classification serves.

As Supreme Court Justice Oliver Wendell Holmes put it:

> It is revolting to have no better reason for a rule of law than that it was so laid down in the time of Henry IV. It is still more revolting if the grounds upon which it was laid down have vanished long since, and the rule simply persists from blind imitation of the past.

O.W. Holmes, "Collected Legal Papers" (Boston, A. Harcourt, 1920), p. 187.

Public policy

Finally, the bill is very bad policy. We are a nation governed by one Constitution. We are not a collection of small nations with contiguous borders. It does not make sense to say to Americans that the existence of their marriages depends on which states they travel through on vacation, or to which states their employer transfers them. Americans have a right to go from state to state, without having to surrender their most intimate relationship as a price of traveling or relocating. Moreover, this bill would create a complex set of legal and logistical problems which have not been fully examined. Since Congress has never sought to do anything of this kind questions about estates, taxes, securities and exchange laws, joint property and shared liability for debt have not been addressed by any of the relevant committees or sponsors of this bill.

As noted above, civil marriage is the way our society defines a person's committed relationships. If one cannot marry his or her partner, the two can be legally ignored and discriminated against in ways, great and small, that would not be tolerated for a moment by the courts if they were married. For example, an unmarried partner can be excluded from the other partner's bedside when crucial medical decisions are made, and even at death. The lack of legal standing may preclude any authority to carry out the partner's wishes.

[The Defense of Marriage Act] discriminates on the basis of sex because it makes one's ability to marry depend on one's gender.

Marriage is the device our society uses to identify partners for virtually every practical situation in which it is important to identify the person who is closest to you. To that end the Supreme Court has held that marriage is a fundamental right. See *Zablocki v. Redhail*, 434 U.S. 374 (1978) (holding that the freedom to marry is a fundamental liberty protected by the Due Process Clause).

The fact that a state allows same-sex couples to marry would not require any religious institution to recognize or perform such marriages. State marriage laws are entirely separate from religious practices in our country. The granting of civil marriage to same-sex couples would not impose any requirements on religious groups, but rather would ensure equal access to the complex structure of rights and responsibilities that *civil* marriage has become.

Marriage is not premised on procreation. See *Griswold v. Connecticut*, 381 U.S. 479 (1965) (right of marital privacy prohibits government from interfering with efforts to actively avoid procreation). In any event, many different-sex couples do not choose or are unable to have children and many same-sex couples do have children.

While marriage has traditionally been defined as a union between people of different sexes, it was also traditionally defined as between people of the same race. As recently as 1967 state governments denied interracial couples the right to marry. *Loving v. Virginia*, 388 U.S. 1 (1967). Marriage was also traditionally understood to involve a man owning a woman as property. We've recognized that these traditions had to be abandoned because they were unfair.

We live in a society which attaches enormous civil, legal consequences to marriage. For example, a person's ability to keep the home she or he has shared with a partner for 20, 30 or more years will depend on their marriage status, especially if they are Medicaid recipients or die intestate. A person's ability to care for a sick or dying partner in most health care facilities depends on whether they are married. Most state laws treat partners who have not married as strangers. It is fundamentally unfair to say on the one hand that you must marry to be treated as next of kin, and then to tell an entire class of Americans who are next of kin in every real sense that they may not marry.

This bill is bad constitutional law and bad policy. For 200 years, Congress has left it to the states to decide who they will marry, and to courts to make sure they respect each other's decisions on that. That is a fine tradition, which ought to be respected. This bill throws it on the trash heap and belittles the relationships of lesbian and gay citizens. Apart from being an unmistakable violation of the Constitution, it is a deplorable act of hostility unworthy of the support.

3

Evidence Suggests That Same-Sex Marriages Were Common in History

Bruce Holsinger

Bruce Holsinger is a writer who specializes in sexuality and cultural politics.

John Boswell's book *Same-Sex Unions in Premodern Europe* gives dozens of examples of church ceremonies from the early Christian era that recognized permanent, romantic, same-sex relationships. The terms "brother," "sister," and "friend," used to describe the new relationships formed by these ceremonies, are equivalents of the modern-day words "lover" or "partner." Same-sex unions in Greco-Roman society were considered to be on an almost equal footing with heterosexual marriages. Criticism of Boswell's book is biased and uninformed.

Gay marriage didn't play in Peoria. On June 11, 1993, the *Journal-Star* of Peoria, Illinois, became one of at least three dailies to announce a temporary ban on Garry Trudeau's *Doonesbury* strip because of the recently out Mark Slackmeyer's blasphemous contention that "for 1,000 years the Church sanctioned rituals for *homosexual* marriages!" The evidence, Mark claims, appears in "a new book by this Yale professor" announcing the discovery of "same-sex ceremonies that included Communion, holy invocations and kissing to signify union."

Same-Sex Unions in Premodern Europe

The Yale historian Mark refers to is John Boswell, and the book is *Same-Sex Unions in Premodern Europe*. In this long-awaited study, Boswell reveals the existence of dozens of ceremonies dating back to the early years of Christianity solemnizing "permanent romantic commitment" between members of the same sex (mostly men) that were "witnessed and recognized by the community." Examples of the ceremony survive in archives

From Bruce Holsinger, "Dearly Beloved." Reprinted with permission from the September 5–12, 1994, issue of the *Nation* magazine.

around Europe and the Near East, from Paris to the island of Patmos to the monastery of St. Catherine on Mount Sinai (delightfully, the Apostolic Library at the Vatican owns twelve of the manuscripts Boswell has uncovered). The rituals appear in many collections alongside heterosexual marriage ceremonies, and the two forms of union are similar enough to suggest "substantial mutual influence or parallel development" throughout the late classical and medieval periods. Although Trudeau's decision to feature *Same-Sex Unions* in his strip certainly did nothing to hamper Villard's publicity efforts, Boswell's book was predictably notorious well before its pub date (it was featured on ABC's *Day One* in the fall of 1993), touching as it does on one of the most hotly contested issues dividing the gay and lesbian community from religious conservatives.

Boswell is no stranger to the controversy over homosexuality in the church. His monumental *Christianity, Social Tolerance, and Homosexuality: Gay People in Western Europe from the Beginning of the Christian Era to the Fourteenth Century*, dubbed one of the eleven best books of 1980 by the *New York Times*, provoked many conservative Catholic scholars by arguing that for a significant portion of its history, Christianity tolerated and even, at certain moments, celebrated male homosexuality. Ironically, the conservative detractors of *CSTH* found vocal allies among a number of gay academics and activists, many of whom were disturbed by what they saw as Boswell's misguided attempt to somehow exonerate the church and Christianity itself from a long history of homophobic oppression.

Anyone familiar with the continuing scholarly and political controversy surrounding *CSTH* will discover that *Same-Sex Unions*, while sharing many of Boswell's earlier concerns, takes a much more cautious approach to written sources and refuses to make unequivocal claims about their meanings and implications. Those hoping for a strident attack on the church will be disappointed; but Boswell's scrupulous and often painstaking sifting of the evidence provides a fascinating read, and the result is a much more convincing study than the book's subject matter might lead one to expect.

Boswell's careful methodology is obvious in the very structure of the book. After a brief introduction, he begins not with the ceremonies themselves but with a comparative study of "the vocabulary of love and marriage" in the modern and premodern West. The author analyzes seemingly uncomplicated terms like "brother," "sister" and "friend," which often functioned in premodern societies as equivalents of the modern "lover" or "partner." A phrase such as "gay marriage," for instance, could be only anachronistically applied to any premodern same-sex union: Not only is the term "gay" steeped in modern connotations but the contemporary Western conception of "marriage" bears only a vague resemblance to comparable ancient and medieval institutions.

The Greco-Roman world

Turning his attention to the Greco-Roman world, Boswell argues that the "*social institution* of heterosexual marriage (as opposed to the personal experience of it, or its religious significance, etc.) has been in most premodern societies primarily a property arrangement," and all major forms of heterosexual union "were strikingly different from superficially similar modern counterparts." Moreover, both Greek and Roman societies were characterized by several forms of "permanent, erotic same-gender" union that were as thoroughly mainstream as their heterosexual counterparts. Boswell argues for a basic continuity from antiquity into the early centuries of Christianity, when same-sex unions were on an almost equal footing with heterosexual matrimony: "The Christian Middle Ages had many reasons to contemn heterosexual arrangements, viewed as a terrestrial convenience or advantage, and at the same time to admire same-sex passion and unions."

From antiquity into the early centuries of Christianity . . . same-sex unions were on an almost equal footing with heterosexual matrimony.

This lengthy excursus (it takes up more than half of his study) provides Boswell with a rich context in which to situate the emergence of the same-sex ceremonies in early Christianity. He cleverly posits the development of heterosexual and same-sex nuptial offices as a single phenomenon, tracking the growth of the latter from "merely a set of prayers" in the earlier Middle Ages to its flowering as a "full office" by the twelfth century that involved "the burning of candles, the placing of the two parties' hands on the Gospel, the joining of their right hands, the binding of their hands . . . with the priest's stole, an introductory litany . . . crowning, the Lord's Prayer, Communion, a kiss, and sometimes circling around the altar." Boswell devotes a full chapter to comparing these rituals with their heterosexual counterparts, revealing a number of extraordinary similarities between the two; in several appendixes totaling almost 100 pages, he has compiled numerous examples of the documents themselves (including heterosexual matrimony ceremonies and adoption rituals for comparison) to let "readers . . . judge for themselves," as he puts it. (Boswell translates most of the ceremonies, so general readers won't have to worry about brushing up on their Old Church Slavonic.)

Boswell tackles head-on the question that most readers will probably be asking themselves: "Was the ceremony 'homosexual' in an erotic sense?" Boswell's answer is once again cautious: "Probably, sometimes, but this is obviously a difficult question to answer about the past, since participants cannot be interrogated. When heterosexual marriages produced children, it is reasonable to assume that they involved sexual intercourse, but in the case of childless heterosexual couples (usually regarded as 'married' by their friends, relatives and neighbors) it is just as difficult to be sure as it is for same-sex pairs." Nevertheless he confidently dismisses the notion that these ceremonies were directed at cementing some form of "blood brotherhood," settling familial disputes or fashioning political alliances: "The same-sex union ceremony makes no mention—in any of its varieties in any language—of tribal, clan, or family loyalty or union: it is unmistakably a voluntary, emotional union of two persons." Boswell stresses that in premodern societies "few people married for erotic fulfillment" anyway; why, he asks implicitly, should same-sex marriages be dismissed on the grounds that they are not demonstrably sexual?

The book's reception

The reception of *Same-Sex Unions* is becoming a story in its own right. Boswell's study may well be construed as a conservative argument for monogamy, and several scholars and religious conservatives have already dismissed it as "advocacy scholarship." Neither charge will be easy to dispel: Boswell himself is a devout Catholic, and he has stated that his work could help people "incorporate [same-sex love] into a Christian lifestyle." Although Boswell clearly presents his work as scholarly rather than political, it has begun to play at least some role in the current controversy over gay marriage: A male couple in Washington, D.C., chose to use one of Boswell's ceremonies for their wedding, and a priest in Hartford who used the rituals to perform a number of gay and lesbian marriages was recently excommunicated.

But if Boswell's book is to have any chance of intervening effectively in this debate (or any other, for that matter), it will first have to survive the slanted treatment it is receiving in the popular press. *Newsweek* is an excellent case in point: Two of the ostensibly objective experts interviewed by staff writer Kenneth Woodward were a Jesuit employed at the Pontifical Oriental Institute in Rome, who claimed that "Boswell has discovered nothing," and a scholar of medieval canon law who had not seen the book but nevertheless felt comfortable labeling Boswell's claims "extremely dubious." When asked how the opinions of a Jesuit working for a Vatican-sanctioned institution might be expected to be more objective than those of any number of gay historians he could have interviewed, Woodward told me he found the question itself "outrageous." While Woodward's review concedes that the ceremonies "resemble rituals the early church used for heterosexual marriages," he notes triumphantly that "the texts make no explicit mention of sex" (and heterosexual ceremonies do?).

In premodern societies "few people married for erotic fulfillment,". . . why . . . should same-sex marriages be dismissed on the grounds that they are not demonstrably sexual?

Newsweek is not alone: *Day One* interviewed two "eminent scholars" for its feature on Boswell who agreed to provide critiques of the book only if guaranteed anonymity. A syndicated *Los Angeles Times* piece quoted an authority on Christian history dismissing the book with the proclamation that "an isolated manuscript or an isolated reference means nothing unless it has corroboration," leaving the clear (and uncorrected) impression that an "isolated manuscript" is all Boswell has. The *Washington Post* ran a vitriolic and condescending review by Camille Paglia, who contends that "Boswell lacks advanced skills in several major areas" and "seems grotesquely incapable of imagining any enthusiasm or intimate bond among men that is not overtly or covertly homosexual."

Despite its fate in print thus far, *Same-Sex Unions*, like *Christianity, Social Tolerance, and Homosexuality*, will unquestionably challenge a number of cherished assumptions about the nature and history of Christianity; once the experts cited in the popular press actually have a chance to read the book, they may find it difficult to dispute Boswell on any but the most technical grounds. In the end, critics will be left with the fact that he has unearthed eighty examples of the ceremony, a staggering figure for anyone aware of the survival rate of medieval manuscripts (Chaucer's *Canterbury Tales*, by comparison, survives in eighty-two manuscripts, *Beowulf* in only one). While the scholarly reception of *Same-Sex Unions*, like that of any groundbreaking study, will certainly be mixed, Boswell's colleagues would do a great service to their profession by publicly challenging the preemptive dismissals of his work in the press and, like Boswell himself, basing their claims on evidence rather than their own preconceptions.

4

Arguments Against Gay Marriage Are Baseless

Scott Bidstrup

Scott Bidstrup is a freelance writer and the founder of Rancho Ambiente, a foster parent home for homeless gay teenagers in southern California.

Most opposition to gay marriage results from the stereotype that gays are sexually promiscuous and unable to form long-term relationships. Gays have relationships that are as permanent and stable as those of straight people. Moreover, gay marriage would not harm children: Studies show that what is most important to children is the love they receive from their parents, not their parents' gender. There are no moral reasons to oppose gay marriage. The real reason people oppose gay marriage is that they are uncomfortable with homosexuality and the idea of gay sex and same-sex marriage.

Ask just about anyone. They'll all tell you they're in favor of equal rights for homosexuals. Just name the situation, and ask. They'll all say, yes, gays should have the same rights in housing, jobs, public accommodations, and should have equal access to government benefits, equal protection of the law, etcetera, etcetera.

Then you get to gay marriage.

And that's when all this talk of equality stops dead cold.

Nearly three people in four in the U.S. oppose gay marriage, almost the same proportion as are otherwise supportive of gay rights. This means that many of the same people who are even passionately in favor of gay rights oppose gays on this one issue.

Why all the passion?

It's because there is a lot of misunderstanding about what homosexuality really is, a lot of stereotypes about gay relationships, and even a great deal of misunderstanding of what marriage itself is all about.

The purpose of this viewpoint is to clear up a few of these misunderstandings and discuss some of the facts surrounding gay relationships and marriage, gay and straight.

First, let's discuss what gay relationships are really all about. The stereotype has it that gays are promiscuous, unable to form lasting relationships, and the relationships that do form are shallow and uncommitted. And gays do have such relationships!

But the important fact to note is that just like in straight society, where such relationships *also* exist, they are a small minority, and exist primarily among the very young. Indeed, one of the most frequent complaints of older gay men is that it is almost impossible to find quality single men to get into a relationship with, because they're already all "taken!"

If you attend any gay event, such as a Pride festival or a PFLAG [Parents, Families and Friends of Lesbians and Gays] convention, you'll find this to be true. As gays age and mature, just like their straight cohorts, they begin to appreciate and find their way into long-term committed relationships.

The values that such gay couples exhibit in their daily lives are often indistinguishable from those of their straight neighbors. They're loyal to their mates, are monogamous, devoted partners. They value and participate in family life, are committed to making their neighborhoods and communities safer and better places to live, and honor and abide by the law. Many make valuable contributions to their communities, serving on school boards, volunteering in community charities, and trying to be good citizens. In doing so, they take full advantage of their relationship to make not only their own lives better, but those of their neighbors as well.

A benefit to heterosexual society of gay marriage is the fact that the commitment of a marriage means the participants are discouraged from promiscuous sex. This has the advantage of slowing the spread of sexually transmitted diseases, which know no sexual orientation and are equal opportunity destroyers.

The values that . . . gay couples exhibit in their daily lives are often indistinguishable from those of their straight neighbors.

These benefits of gay marriage have changed the attitudes of the majority of people in Denmark and other countries where various forms of gay marriage have been legal for years. Indeed, in 1989, when the proposal to legalize marriage between gays first was proposed in Denmark, the majority of the clergy were opposed. Now, after having seen the benefits to the partners and to society, they are overwhelmingly in favor, according to the surveys done then and now.

So, having established the value of gay marriage, why are people so opposed to it?

Many of the reasons offered for opposing gay marriage are based on the assumption that gays have a choice in who they can feel attracted to, and the reality is quite different. Many people actually believe that gays could simply choose to be heterosexual if they wished. But the reality is that very few do have a choice—any more than very few heterosexuals could choose which sex to find themselves attracted to.

Additionally, many people continue to believe that homosexuality is about nothing but sex, considering it to be merely a sexual perversion. The reality is that homosexuality is multidimensional, and is much more about love and affection than it is about sex. And this is what gay relationships are based on—mutual attraction, love and affection. Sex is a means of expressing that love, just the same as it is for heterosexuals. Being gay is much more profound than simply a sexual relationship; being gay is part of that person's core identity, and goes right to the very center of his being. It's like being black in a society of whites, or a blonde European in a nation of black-haired Asians. Yes, being gay is just that profound to the person who is. This is something that few heterosexuals can understand unless they are a minority themselves.

The arguments against gay marriage

Well, of course there are a lot of reasons being offered these days for opposing gay marriage, and they are usually variations on a few well-established themes. Interestingly, a court in Hawaii has recently heard them all. And it found, after due deliberation, that they didn't hold water. Here's a summary:

1. Marriage is an institution between one man and one woman. Well, that's the most often heard argument, one even codified in U.S. federal law. Yet it is easily the weakest. *Who* says who marriage is to be defined by? The married? The marriable? Isn't that kind of like allowing a banker to decide who is going to own the money stored in his vaults? It seems to me that if the straight community cannot show a compelling reason to *deny* the institution of marriage to gay people, it shouldn't be denied. And such simple, nebulous declarations are hardly a compelling reason. They're really more like an expression of prejudice than any kind of a real argument. The concept of not denying people their rights unless you can show a compelling reason to do so is the very basis of the American ideal of human rights.

2. Marriage is for procreation. The proponents of that argument are really hard pressed to explain why, if that's the case, infertile couples are allowed to marry. I, for one, would love to be there when the proponent of such an argument is to explain to his post-menopausal mother or impotent father that since they cannot procreate, they must now surrender their wedding rings! That would be fun to watch! Again, such an argument fails to persuade based on the marriages society does allow routinely, without even a second thought.

3. Same-sex couples aren't the optimum environment in which to raise children. That's an interesting one, in light of who society *does* allow to get married and bring children into their marriage. Check it out: murderers, convicted felons of all sorts, *even known child molesters* are all allowed to freely marry and procreate, and do so every day, with hardly a second thought by these same critics. So if children are truly the priority here, why is this allowed? The fact is that many gay couples raise children, adopted and occasionally their own from failed attempts at heterosexual marriages. Lots and lots of scientific studies have shown that the outcomes of the children raised in the homes of gay and lesbian couples are just as good as those of straight couples. The differences have been shown again and again to be insignificant. Psychologists tell us that what makes the difference is the *love* of the parents, not their gender. The studies are very clear about that. And gay people are as capable of loving children as fully as anyone else.

4. *Gay relationships are immoral.* Says who? The Bible? Somehow, I always thought that freedom of religion *implied* the right to freedom *from* religion as well. The Bible has absolutely no standing in American law, and because it doesn't, no one has the right to impose rules on anyone else simply because of something they perceive to be mandated by the Bible. Not all world religions have a problem with homosexuality; many sects of Buddhism, for example, celebrate gay relationships freely and would like to have the authority to make them legal marriages. In that sense, *their* religious freedom is being infringed. If one believes in religious freedom, the recognition that opposition to gay marriage is based on religious arguments is reason enough to discount this argument.

5. *Marriages are for ensuring the continuation of the species.* The proponents of such an argument are going to have a really hard time persuading me that the human species is in any real danger of dying out through lack of procreation. If ten percent of all the human race were to suddenly refrain from procreation, I think it is safe to say that the world would probably be better off. One of the world's most serious problems is overpopulation and the increasing anarchy that is resulting from it. Seems to me that gays would be doing the world a favor by not bringing more hungry mouths into an already overburdened world. So why encourage them?

6. *Same-sex marriage would threaten the institution of marriage.* That one's contradictory right on the face of it. Threaten marriage? By allowing people to marry? That doesn't sound very logical to me. If you allow gay people to marry each other, you no longer encourage them to marry people to whom they feel little attraction, with whom they most often cannot relate sexually, and thereby reduce the number of supposed heterosexual marriages that end up in the divorce courts. If it is the institution of heterosexual marriage that worries you, then consider that no one would require you or anyone else to participate in a gay marriage. So you would have freedom of choice, of choosing what kind of marriage to participate in—something more than what you have now. And speaking of divorce—to argue that the institution of marriage is worth preserving at the cost of requiring involuntary participants to remain in it is a better argument for tightening divorce laws than proscribing gay marriage.

Lots of scientific studies have shown that the outcomes of the children raised in the homes of gay and lesbian couples are just as good as those of straight couples.

---

7. *Marriage is traditionally a heterosexual institution.* This is morally the weakest argument. Slavery was also a traditional institution, based on traditions that went back to the very beginnings of human history. But by the 19th century, humankind had realized the evils of that institution, and has since largely abolished it. Why not recognize the truth—that there is no moral ground on which to support the tradition of marriage

as a strictly heterosexual institution, and remove the restriction?

8. *Same-sex marriage is an untried social experiment.* The American critics of same-sex marriage betray their provincialism with this argument. The fact is that a form of gay marriage has been legal in Denmark since 1989 (full marriage rights except for adoption rights and church weddings, and a proposal now exists in the Danish parliament to allow both of those rights as well), and most of the rest of Scandinavia from not long after. Full marriage rights have existed in many Dutch cities for several years. In other words, we have a long-running "experiment" to examine for its results—which have uniformly been positive. Opposition to the Danish law was led by the clergy (much the same as in the States). A survey conducted at the time revealed that 72 percent of Danish clergy were opposed to the law. It was passed anyway, and the change in the attitude of the clergy there has been dramatic—a survey conducted in 1995 indicated that 89 percent of the Danish clergy now admit that the law is a good one and has had many beneficial effects, including a reduction in suicide, in the spread of sexually transmitted diseases and in promiscuity and infidelity among gays. Far from leading to the "destruction of Western civilization" as some critics (including the Mormon and Catholic churches) have warned, the result of the "experiment" has actually been civilizing and strengthening, not just to the institution of marriage, but to society as a whole. So perhaps we should accept the fact that someone else has already done the "experiment" and accept the results.

The *real* reasons people oppose gay marriage

So far, we've examined the reasons everyone gives for opposing gay marriage. Let's examine now the *real* reasons people oppose it:

Just not comfortable with the idea. The fact that people aren't comfortable with the idea stems primarily from the fact that for many years, society has promoted the idea that a marriage between members of the same sex is ludicrous, mainly because of the objections raised above. But if those objections don't make sense, neither does the idea that gay marriage is necessarily ludicrous.

It offends everything religion stands for. Whose religion? Many mainstream Christian denominations, to be sure, and definitely most branches of Islam and Orthodox Judaism, but outside those, most religions are unopposed to gay marriage, and many actually favor it. When the Mormon church arrogantly claimed to represent all religions in the *Baehr vs. Lewin* trial in Hawaii, the principal Buddhist sect in that state made it very clear that the Mormon church didn't represent *them*, and made it very clear that they support the right of gay couples to marry. That particular Buddhist sect claims many more members in Hawaii than does the Mormon church. In a society that claims to offer religious freedom, the use of the power of the state to enforce private religious sensibilities is an affront to all who would claim the right to worship according to the dictates of their own conscience.

Making love to another man betrays everything that is macho. Well, I've known (and dated) plenty of very masculine gay men in my day, including a Hell's Angel biker type, who, if you suggested he is a limp-wristed fairy, would likely rip your head off and hand it to you. There was a long-honored tradition of gay relationships among the tough and macho cowboys of the Old West. Plenty of masculine, respected movie stars are gay. Indeed, Rock Hudson was considered the very *archetype* of a masculine man. Came as quite a shock to a lot of macho-men to find out he was gay! So what's wrong with all these kinds of men expressing love for each other? Is that so wrong? A society that devalues love devalues that upon which civilized society is based. Should *any* form of that love be discouraged?

The arguments against gay marriage don't hold up to close scrutiny.

The thought of gay sex is repulsive. Well, it will come as some surprise to a lot of heterosexuals to find out that, to a lot of gays, the thought of *heterosexual sex* is repulsive! But does that mean the discomfort of some gays to heterosexual couples should be a reason to deny heterosexuals the right to marry? I don't think so, even though the thought of a man kissing a woman is rather repulsive to many homosexuals! Well then, why should it work the other way? Besides, the same sexual practices that gays engage in are often engaged in by heterosexual couples anyway. Prompting the ever-popular gay T-shirt: "SO-DO-MY—SO DO MY neighbors, SO DO MY friends."

A civil rights issue

When gay people say that this is a civil rights issue, we are referring to matters like the fact that we cannot make medical decisions for our partners in an emergency. Instead, the hospitals are usually forced by state laws to go to the families who may be estranged from us for decades, who are often hostile to us, and totally ignore our wishes for the treatment of our partners. If that hostile family wishes to exclude us from the hospital room, they may legally do so in nearly all cases.

If our partners are arrested, we can be compelled to testify against them, which legally married couples are not forced to do.

In many cases, even carefully drawn wills and durable powers of attorney have frequently proven to not be enough if a family wishes to challenge a will, overturn a custody decision, or exclude us from a funeral or deny us the right to visit a partner's grave. As survivors, they can even seize a real estate property that we may have been buying together for years, quickly sell it at a huge loss and stick us with the remaining debt on a property we no longer own.

These aren't just theoretical issues, either; they happen with surprising frequency. Almost any older gay couple can tell you stories of friends who have been victimized in such ways.

These are all civil rights issues that have nothing whatever to do with the ecclesiastical origins of marriage; they are matters that have become enshrined in state laws over the years in many ways that exclude us from the rights that legally married couples enjoy and consider their right. This is why we say it is very much a civil rights issue; it has nothing to do with who performs the ceremony or whether an announcement is accepted for publication in the local paper. It is not a matter of "special rights" to ask for the same rights that other couples enjoy by law, even by constitutional mandate.

As we have seen, the arguments against gay marriage don't hold up to close scrutiny. Neither the arguments traditionally raised nor the real feelings of the opponents make much sense when held up to the light of reason.

So let's get on with it. Let's get over our aversion to what we oppose for silly, irrational reasons, based on ignorance and faulty assumptions, and make ours a more just and honorable society, finally honoring that last phrase from the Pledge of Allegiance; "With liberty and justice for all."

5

Lesbians and Gay Men Should Fight for the Freedom to Marry

Evan Wolfson

Evan Wolfson is the senior staff attorney and director of the Marriage Project for the Lambda Legal Defense and Education Fund, a gay-rights organization. He also served as cocounsel for the gay-marriage case Baehr v. Lewin *(renamed* Baehr v. Miike *in 1996) in Hawaii.*

Prohibiting same-sex marriage deprives gays and lesbians of the fundamental right to marry. It also denies them hundreds of legal, social, economic, and practical benefits that derive from the institution of marriage. Laws denying same-sex couples the right to marry are similar to previous laws that forbade couples of different races to marry. In order to achieve true equality, lesbians and gay men must fight for nothing less than their equal right to enjoy all the benefits that marriage confers.

Imagine if tomorrow, by act of law, lesbians and gay men were denied the right to raise children together in a protected relationship[1] or to have their committed relationships recognized and given benefits such as annuities, pension plans, Social Security, and Medicare.[2] Or if by act of law, same-sex couples who had lived together for the longest time were not allowed joint filing of tax returns, joint insurance policies for home, auto, and health, or access during dissolution or divorce to protections such as community property and child support.[3]

Imagine how you would feel if you and your partner were told that, because of that act of law, you had to choose between love and country because your same-sex relationship was not respected for immigration and residency.[4] Or that the act of law meant that your partner's death left you without rights of inheritance, protection against eviction from the home you had shared, exemption from oppressive taxation, or even bereavement leave.[5] Imagine that the act of law stamped you as unqualified to make decisions about your partner's health or medical treatment, or

From Evan Wolfson, "Why We Should Fight for the Freedom to Marry: The Challenges and Opportunities That Will Follow a Win in Hawaii," *Journal of Gay, Lesbian, and Bisexual Identity*, vol. 1, no. 1, 1996. Reprinted by permission of the author and publisher, Human Sciences Press, a division of Plenum Publishing Corporation.

even her or his funeral arrangements.[6] Or that the act of law branded you as permanent sexual outlaws, unequal citizens, and even not fully human—because of the gender of the person you love.[7]

In fact, that act of law has already happened; it's called "same-sex couples can't get married." All this unequal treatment and more is already there, because in all 50 states, lesbians and gay men are denied the basic human right, the constitutional freedom, to marry.[8]

Because literally hundreds of important legal, economic, practical, and social benefits and protections flow directly from marriage,[9] the exclusion from this central social institution wreaks real harm on real-life same-sex couples every day. From lesbian mothers denied custody of their children or the right to adopt their partners' children (case after case), to gay men literally separated at the INS [Immigration and Naturalization Service] office because they could not find a country that would allow them to live together (case after case), to gay people out in the cold when a relationship ended, or unable to get an order of protection against domestic violence when the relationship went sour—the denial of marriage rights has been a stone wall against which we have run up again and again.

Today the movement and its allies face critical choices. Do we work not just to *win* the freedom to marry (which we are likely to do), but to *keep* it (against the coming backlash)? Or do we fail to organize, fail to do the necessary political organizing and coalition-building, fail to get out front and frame the debate in our way—and thus miss a vital opportunity to engage the public and educate the world about our family relationships? Will we get so caught up in our own intracommunity discussions about "redefining the family," or our own all-or-nothing rhetoric, that we are once again caught unprepared for the actual legal, political, and cultural battles soon to be unfolding in every state, this time around the galvanizing question of whether gay people should be able to keep the freedom to marry we hopefully will win in Hawaii?

Lambda's [Lambda Legal Defense and Education Fund] landmark case in Hawaii, *Baehr v. Lewin*,[10] seems headed toward victory. The battle over marriage rights and lesbians and gay relationships is heading toward unprecedented national dimensions, front-page headlines, courts, and legislatures in every state. Will we pull together and prepare, or will we miss the boat?

The similarities with same-race restrictions

Although no discrimination is exactly the same, and there is no reason to get into an argument over some "hierarchy of oppression,"[11] there are many analogies to be drawn from this nation's previous experience in excluding people from the institution of marriage. For example, Stephanie Smith of the National Center for Lesbian Rights/Lesbians of Color Project has spoken eloquently of the parallels between the "different-sex restriction" still in force against gay and lesbian people's choice of a marital partner and the "same-race restriction" that less than 30 years ago prevented interracial couples from marrying.[12]

Consider this law imposing a "same-race restriction" on marriage struck down (only twenty-nine years ago!) by the U.S. Supreme Court in *Loving v. Virginia* (1967)[13]: "All marriages between a white person and a colored person shall be absolutely *void* without any decree of divorce or other legal process." Notice how closely it resembles the equally offensive and unconstitutional bill imposing a "different-sex restriction" on marriage, recently proposed in South Dakota: "Any marriage between persons of the same gender is null and *void* from the beginning."[14]

In *Loving*, a black woman and a white man were criminally convicted for violating Virginia's miscegenation law, which imposed a "same-race restriction" on marriage. Exiling(!) the Lovings from their home state for 25 years and declaring their marriage "void," the trial judge stated,

> Almighty God created the races white, black, yellow, malay, and red, and he placed them on separate continents. . . . The fact that he separated the races shows that he did not intend for the races to mix.[15]

The Supreme Court struck down this "same-race restriction" on marital choice as a "measure . . . designed to maintain White Supremacy." In much the same way, the "different-sex restriction" deprives gay and lesbian people of a basic human right and brands us as inferior, second-class citizens, thus justifying and reinforcing stereotypes and prejudice as well as other discrimination.

In all 50 states, lesbians and gay men are denied the basic human right, the constitutional freedom, to marry.

People today forget how the language now being used against same-sex couples' equal marriage rights not so long ago was used against interracial couples—denying people's equal human dignity and freedom to share in the rights and responsibilities of marriage. Today, you even hear some *gay* and *lesbian* people saying that the fact that marriage is today denied to same-sex couples shows that it is intrinsically heterosexual, ignoring the fact that marriage (like other social institutions we are part of or seek to make our own choices whether or not to be part of) has changed throughout history to meet the needs and values of real people.[16]

Now imagine if the Lovings had been told that instead of challenging this discrimination and fighting for their right to marry, they should instead devote their limited resources solely to unhooking benefits and protections from marriage. Or if the lawyers working on their case from the ACLU [American Civil Liberties Union] and the Japanese-American Citizens League [both of which have endorsed Lambda's Marriage Resolution calling for equal marriage rights for gay people[17]] had said that we should not work on ending the ban on interracial marriage until we achieve universal health care.

Would anyone say that people in love should accept discrimination based on their race or religion until other injustices are rectified? Or would we say that *both* the discrimination and the other injustices should be combatted and that those like the Lovings are right to challenge their exclusion from a central social institution? Would we counsel the Lovings to accept unequal treatment, or even "separate-but-equal"? And if we wouldn't, why should people facing discrimination based on their gender or sexual orientation, or the gender or sexual orientation of the person they love most, have to accept it either?

Many gay people do not realize how denial [of the right to marry] directly deprives us of a litany of benefits and protections, rights and responsibilities.

History is upon us. For many, perhaps most, gay and nongay people, marriage is important in its own right. Regardless, marriage is now also a vehicle, a forum, a venue for the titanic battles at hand. And each of us, every organization, must decide: Am I going to be a part of this battle, are we fighting to win, or am I going to sit this one out or focus elsewhere? Unquestionably, there is much work and many issues that are important. Yet saying "Let's not work for this" is in effect saying "You should not have this," for, as Martin Luther King, Jr. instructs, "It is a historical fact that privileged groups seldom give up their privileges voluntarily. . . . Freedom is never voluntarily given by the oppressor; it must be demanded by the oppressed."[18]

I believe that the cultural, political, and legal battles about to erupt over our freedom to marry require us to seize the challenge and opportunity by beginning to prepare NOW. What is that opportunity, and what must we do?

The coming (and inevitable) battles over marriage will give us the opportunity to educate the nation about the reality and diversity of lesbian and gay lives and family relationships. We can tell true and compelling stories about who we are; what our needs are as couples, as parents, as partners, as people; and how the denial of the right to marry harms us. We can tell of the lesbians and gay men of color in our communities, the economically disadvantaged, the religiously oriented, the parents, the long-term partners "in sickness and in health," the functional families, the rural and domestic—all injured in tangible and intangible ways by being denied their freedom to define their own family and make their own choice about marriage.

This fight and the stakes cut across race, gender, and class lines.[19] For decades, the radical right has been campaigning against, and mischaracterizing, our desire and need for equal marriage rights;[20] it is time that we, too, started talking about it, framing the discussion accurately and compellingly.

The Marriage Resolution

What can people do? To me it boils down to the nitty-gritty work of social change: engaging people through education and asking for their support. We must give a wake-up call and a heads-up to ourselves and our allies, and create a climate of receptivity among others. To that end, Lambda and other groups have created the Marriage Resolution:

> Because marriage is a basic human right and an individual personal choice, RESOLVED, the State should not interfere

with same-gender couples who choose to marry and share fully and equally in the rights, responsibilities, and commitment of civil marriage.

The Marriage Resolution is a vehicle for (a) promoting the necessary discussion and consideration of our equal marriage rights among gay and nongay people (and organizations), (b) collecting signatories to build and demonstrate a growing coalition (Lambda to be a central repository, with list to be shared), and (c) giving people a tool and a task in building that coalition and approaching others.

By asking any organization you belong to or feel comfortable approaching to consider and adopt the Resolution, you are moving people and helping forge a coalition that can snowball. With the Marriage Resolution and materials from Lambda, GLAAD [Gay and Lesbian Alliance Against Defamation], NGLTF [National Gay and Lesbian Task Force], NCLR [National Center for Lesbian Rights], and others, everyone can become a one-person wave of activism toward friends, families, allies, and organizations. We can firm up our supporters, while softening up the initially hostile or uninformed, but *reachable* mass of most Americans.

Nor is it just nongay people who need education about lesbian and gay families. Many gay people do not know that we are denied the right to marry; many gay people do not realize how denial directly deprives us of a litany of benefits and protections, rights and responsibilities. And many people do not understand just how false a choice it is to be presented with the question, "Should we work for marriage, or for domestic partnership?"[21] [Domestic partnerships grant to homosexual and unmarried couples some of the legal and economic benefits previously awarded only to married couples.]

I do not believe lesbians and gay men who wish to marry should be denied that freedom, that equality, that choice, simply because of who they are or whom they love.

First, there is nothing antithetical about believing that gay people should be able to exercise the equal right to marry and, at the same time, believing that other family forms—including perhaps, but not limited to, domestic partnership—are valuable and should be treated fairly. We know this because at Lambda, we litigated and won benefits for gay and nongay unmarried partners of city employees in New York[22] and continue to press other "domestic partnership" cases.

Some say that if gay men and lesbians were allowed to marry, "the entire domestic-partnership movement would dry up tomorrow. . . ."[23] Of course, either this is untrue or it is a revealing insight into the lesbian and gay community's relative support for marriage, vis-à-vis domestic partnership, once given a meaningful option (as we will have been, when the Hawaii Supreme Court hands down its final ruling). If the assertion were true, would the proper course for the movement be to foist domestic partnership on those who would prefer a choice regarding marriage? Is losing marriage as an option (after we win it in Hawaii or elsewhere) an acceptable price to pay for fueling the domestic partnership "movement"?

Of course, we need not assume the assertion to be true. Clearly there are many of us committed to meeting the needs of all families and individuals without sole regard to marriage. But I do not believe lesbians and gay men who wish to marry should be denied that freedom, that equality, that choice, simply because of who they are or whom they love.

Second, although the recent trend toward adopting domestic partnership ordinances and policies locality by locality, and increasing efforts to equalize access to employment benefits company by company, are welcome and important innovations, we should keep one thing clear: domestic partnership is not marriage. Allowing lesbians and gay men access only to domestic partnerships, while reserving marriage for different-sex couples, is a form of second-class citizenship, and perpetuates discrimination.

And, despite the hard work and best intentions of many activists,[24] it is indeed second-class. For one thing, "domestic partnership" has become kind of a shorthand phrase for a variety of different means of winning some slice of benefits and/or recognition for unmarried couples; it means different things to different people, ranging from voluntary company policies on benefits, to civic registries, to a hypothesized flexible family form. Domestic partnership does not *exist* as a unitary "thing" or national institution, unlike marriage, which is recognized across state lines and at every level of society. Moreover, not only is domestic partnership unequal to marriage in the sense that "separate but equal is inherently unequal," but under the domestic partnership ordinances and policies adopted so far, the benefits on their own terms are not equal to those provided to married partners.

The obligations, but not the benefits

For example, many of the ordinances require domestic partners to undertake the responsibilities and legal obligations that accompany marriage, but do not in exchange give domestic partners even most of the benefits of marriage. Nor do they provide equal recognition. The ordinances, because local, do not—and could not—assure domestic partners the full range of benefits extended married partners at the state level; even were a state to adopt statewide domestic partnership, it would be unable to deliver *federal* and out-of-state benefits and protections. The ordinances do not—and most likely, under federal law, could not—mandate that private employers treat domestic partners the same as married partners; even the 30 or so cities and the 2 states[25] that have the best domestic partnership programs at most provide health benefits only to *government* employees. The ordinances do not—and are not permitted to—provide domestic partners parental protections and benefits that are provided to married partners.

Arguably, the greatest success of the "domestic partnership" "movement" has been persuading many private universities and companies *voluntarily* to give their gay and lesbian employees (and it is *almost always* restricted to gay and lesbian) some of the benefits given their married employees.[26] When challenged in court, whether in Colorado[27] or California,[28] Massachusetts,[29] Minnesota,[30] Wisconsin,[31] or more recently,

Georgia,[32] domestic partnership has almost always lost.

At the same time, ironically, under most, if not all of these laws, the criteria for establishing a domestic partnership are far more onerous than those imposed on a couple seeking to marry. Thus, on the one hand, domestic partnership fails to resonate with the emotional and declarative (and often religious) power most people feel inheres in marriage. On the other hand, domestic partnership fails to "redefine the family" or "equalize access" to benefits, because it is hampered by legal obstacles and by the need to define it as a status so as to, once again, exclude people not in a sufficiently committed, interdependent, or caretaking relationship. Why is it somehow correct to fight for domestic partnership or accept it as a step toward something else, while incorrect to make the same calculus with regard to (the far more resonant, potent, and benefit-laden institution of) marriage?

Allowing lesbians and gay men access only to domestic partnerships, while reserving marriage for different-sex couples, is a form of second-class citizenship.

The domestic partnership approach is a healthy step toward eliminating marital status discrimination and arbitrariness in the recognition of valuable family relationships. Recognizing "domestic partnerships" or adopting policies equalizing access to benefits is likely to be one of the best steps available to a locality, private institution, company, or university—as distinguished from a state. Such steps help demonstrate the marital nature, the spousal equivalence, of gay and lesbian relationships, while at the same time showing the absence of any legitimate, let alone compelling, State interest in disparate treatment or segregated status. But, ultimately, domestic partnership alone is not enough. As feminist columnist Anna Quindlen put it in coming out for equal marriage rights,

> there is no secular reason that we should take a patchwork approach of corporate, governmental, and legal steps to guarantee what can be done simply, economically, conclusively, and inclusively with the words, "I do."[33]

Our demand as gay and lesbian people for equal choices and recognition with regard to our family relationships does not undermine our demand as conscientious citizens to decouple benefits from arbitrary criteria of any kind. But, equally, our desire to achieve a more just, contextual allocation of benefits should not require us to accept an inferior status with regard to marriage or other choices. The couples in Hawaii—Ninia and Genora, Pat and Joe—are just as entitled as anyone to decide for themselves how to define their families and live their lives.

A few marriage critics express a concern that winning the right to marry may somehow "delegitimiz[e] some of us in the eyes of other gays and lesbians in the name of legitimizing all of us in the eyes of heterosexuals."[34] This will be true only if "we" let it be true. As Professor Ruthann Robson, no supporter of equal marriage rights, frankly concedes, "legalized lesbian marriage would not invent the good lesbian/deviant lesbian dichotomy."[35] It is our job as activists not to conflate rhetoric with reality, not to confuse tactics with objectives, and not to rely on one vehicle or voice to achieve the full social change we want. We must see opportunities in challenges, while always tactically advancing so as to, at least, *lose* forward.

In my view, it is telling that the one state in the country where there is any serious discussion about legislative adoption of a "comprehensive" statewide domestic partnership law is Hawaii. And it's no coincidence that that discussion, and that serious possibility, has opened up only in response to the likely victory in our case and the coalition-building, education, and organizing that have accompanied our fight over marriage rights.

The battles over equal marriage rights *are* coming. They will be fought, not just in Hawaii, but in every state and in Washington, D.C. Every lesbian and gay issue and community will be affected by those battles; every issue and community stands to benefit or be harmed, depending in part on how we seize the opportunity and begin preparing now. There will be victories and setbacks; we must persevere through both over the long haul. We must use the battleline of marriage as a powerful opportunity to advance on many fronts, and to tell the truth about who we are and how we love.

In three states, we have seen the backlash against equality begin before we have even "lashed," before we have even won the equal right to marry. In Utah, South Dakota, and Alaska, radical-right legislators introduced antimarriage legislation aimed preemptively at thwarting recognition of marriages we someday may lawfully celebrate in Hawaii or elsewhere.[36] The results of these opening skirmishes are revealing. In Utah, by cheating, the bill passed through the legislature and became law.[37] In Alaska, it is too soon to predict. [The bill became law in the spring of 1996.]

It is time to demand full, full, full equality, and to tell the truth about who we are and what we want for ourselves and our loved ones.

But in South Dakota, thanks to the hard work of local activists together with NGLTF and Lambda, we won.[38] In round 1, the legislature rejected the assault on our equal right to marry and see those marriages recognized throughout the nation, just as other lawful marriages are. This victory came even before we had a chance to organize, prepare, build a coalition, ask for support, and frame the discussion. It offers us hope: we *can* win.

We have not yet begun to fight. It is time to demand full, full, full equality, and to tell the truth about who we are and what we want for ourselves and our loved ones. Although no one victory (be it marriage, antidiscrimination laws, or the right to adopt) is the end of our fight, you cannot be for "equality" while acquiescing in the denial of so fundamental a freedom as the *equal* right to choose whether and whom to marry. We may never all agree on marriage or any other single issue or vehicle. But we at Lambda and the many others who are joining us in this effort believe that the coming battles around marriage will affect far more than just ("just"!) the freedom to marry. What we need for now is less "point/counterpoint" and more ways for all of us, and our allies, to pull together.

Gay and lesbian people want the right to choose whether and whom to marry for the same mix of personal, economic, and practical reasons that nongay people do. As Lambda's landmark case in Hawaii progresses toward a much-hoped-for and anticipated victory, we must educate ourselves and others about the importance of, and need for, equal marriage rights for lesbians and gay men. Anticipating and seizing the opportunities that the marriage battles will engender, we must get to work—now.

Notes

1. See, e.g., *Matter of Dana*, No. 93-0747 (2d Dep't Apr. 3, 1995) (nonbiological mother not permitted to adopt partner's child without cutoff of parental rights because they are not married).

2. See, e.g., *Bagley v. California Federal Bank*, No. CV 93-7027MRP (C.D. Cal. Mar. 3, 1995) (unmarried gay couple not permitted to have employee loan discount available to married nongay couple).

3. See, e.g., Anne Stroock, "Gay Divorces Complicated by Lack of Laws," *S.F. Chronicle*, May 14, 1990, at A4 (denial of parental rights to non-biological parent one of the consequences wrought by the denial of marriage rights to same-sex partners); Kirk Johnson, "Gay Divorce: Few Markers in This Realm," *N.Y. Times*, Aug. 12, 1994, at A20 ("Because gay people cannot be legally married in the United States, there is, for starters, no access to divorce court.").

4. E.g., *Sullivan v. INS*, 772 F.2d 609 (9th Cir. 1984) (noncitizen partner in long-term gay couple denied right to remain with his partner in United States because not married); see also Kimberly Griffin, "To Have and to Hold: Gay Marriage, the Next Frontier," *Windy City Times*, June 2, 1994, 1, at 46 (stories of binational couples facing prospect of separation because unable to marry and remain together legally).

5. E.g., *Brinkin v. Southern Pac. Transp. Co.*, 572 ESupp. 236 (N.D. Cal. 1983) (death of partner after 11 years together does not qualify employee for bereavement leave).

6. E.g. In re. *Guardianship of Sharon Kowalski*, 382 N.W.2d 861 (Minn. 1986), *reversed*, 478 N.W.2d 790 (Minn In re. . . 1991).

7. See, generally, Evan Wolfson & Robert S. Mower, "When the Police Are in Our Bedrooms, Shouldn't the Courts Go in After Them?" An Update on the Fight Against 'Sodomy' Laws," 21 *Fordham Urb. L.J.* 997 (1994).

8. See *Baehr v. Lewin*, 852 P.2d 44, 59 (1993) (Hawaii Supreme Court describes the "encyclopedic" "multiplicity of rights and benefits that are contingent upon [marital] status"); see also *Van Dyck v. Van Dyck*, 425 S.E.2d 853 (Ga. 1993) (Sears-Collins, J., concurring).

9. See Richard D. Mohr, "The Case for Gay Marriage," 9 *Notre Dame J. Law, Ethics Pub. Pol.* 215, 227–228 (1995); Craig A. Bowman & Blake M. Cornish, "A More Perfect Union: A Legal and Social Analysis of Domestic Partnership Ordinances," 92 *Colum. L. Rev.* 1164, 1167–1168 (1992).

10. 852 P.2d 44, 75 (Haw. 1993). For a discussion of this epochal case and its implications, see, e.g., Evan Wolfson, "Crossing the Threshold: Equal Marriage Rights for Lesbians and Gay Men, and the Intra-Community

Critique," 21 *N.Y.U. Rev. L. Soc. Change* 567, 572–581 (1994) (hereinafter: "Crossing the Threshold").

11. Henry Louis Gates, Jr., "Blacklash," *The New Yorker*, May 11, 1993, at 42–43 ("trying to establish a pecking order of oppression is generally a waste of time").

12. Michelangelo Signorile, "Wedding Bell Blues," *Out Magazine*, May 1995, at 26 (quoting Smith's remarks to the 1995 Black Gay & Lesbian Leadership Forum Summit in Los Angeles, at which she described how her own parents had to leave their home state of Missouri to find a state that would marry them).

13. 388 U.S. 1 (1967) (striking down Virginia's same-race restriction on an individual's choice of marital partner).

14. H.B. 1184, "An Act to prohibit a marriage between persons of the same gender" (1995). Saying that either an interracial or a same-sex couple's marriage is "void" means more than that a court may choose not to recognize such a marriage; it means that "by definition," it is not a marriage.

15. 388 U.S. at 3; see "Crossing the Threshold" at 575–576.

16. "Crossing the Threshold" at 588–591.

17 See, infra, at 82 for discussion of the Marriage Resolution. A list of signatories is available through Lambda Legal Defense & Education Fund, 666 Broadway, New York, NY 10012, which organizations may also contact to sign on. On the JACL's endorsement of equal marriage rights, see Gerard Lim, "JACL Formally Adopts Same-Sex Marriage," *AsianWeek*, Aug. 12, 1994, at 7.

18 Martin Luther King, Jr., *Why We Can't Wait*, at 80. In a similar vein, the Jewish scholar, Rabbi Hillel, instructed, "If I am not for myself, who will be?" We must demand our full equality, specifically including the freedom to marry; our opponents will certainly be mentioning marriage.

19. "People had never really thought of gay marriage as a 'people of color' issue. [But following presentations at the Black Lesbian & Gay Leadership Forum Summit,] everyone started talking about talking to their ministers, their parents, their neighbors. They began seeing that this is not about class and privilege and a bunch of rich people flying off to Hawaii. It's about defining what a family is to each of us." "Wedding Bell Blues" at 26 (quoting NCLR's Smith).

20. "Crossing the Threshold" at 595–596.

21. The following discussion of "domestic partnership" is drawn from a fuller treatment in "Crossing the Threshold" at 604–608; see also the discussion of the stakes and limitations in domestic partnership in Bowman & Cornish, *passim*.

22. See *Gay Teachers Ass'n v. Bd. of Educ.*, No. 43069/88 (N.Y. Sup. Ct. Aug. 12, 1991), *aff'd*, 585 N.Y.S. 2d 1016 (N.Y. App. Div. May 12, 1992) (successful settlement, Oct. 30, 1993, on file with Lambda).

23. See Chris Bull, "Till Death Do Us Part," *The Advocate*, Nov. 30, 1993, at 40, 46 (quoting activist).

24. I include myself in this, for I have litigated "domestic partnership" cases and have urged it as a strategy for winning recognition and benefits for more families, facilitating people's ability to define their families and see

their needs addressed fairly. But it is not a substitute for the freedom to marry, nor need we present it as such.

25. Vermont and New York provide access to certain benefits to unmarried state workers and their partners.

26. See, e.g., David Jefferson, "Gay Employees Win Benefits for Partners at More Corporations," *Wall St. Journal*, Mar. 18, 1994, p. A1, col. 1. To get a periodic reporting of the latest companies and jurisdictions providing some benefits and/or recognition to unmarried couples, see *Lesbian & Gay Law Ass'n, Lesbian/Gay Law Notes* (Prof. Arthur S. Leonard, Ed.) (monthly publication).

27. *Ross v. Denver Dep't of Health & Hospitals*, 883 P.2d 516 (Colo. Ct. App. 1994).

28. *Hinman v. Dep't of Personnel Administration*, 213 Cal. Rptr 410, 419–20 (Ct. App. 1985).

29. *Huff v. Chapel Hill. Chauney Hall*, No. 93-BEM-1041 (Mass. Comm'n Against Discrim'n Sept. 14, 1994).

30 *Lilly v. City of Minneapolis*, 527 NW2d 107, *rev. denied*,-NW2d-(Mar. 31, 1995).

31. *Phillips v. Wisc. Personnel Comm'n*, 482 NW2d 121 (Wis. Ct. App. 1992).

32. *City of Atlanta v. McKinney*, 1995 WL 116312 (Ga. S. Ct. Mar. 14, 1995).

33. Anna Quindlen, "Evan's Two Moms," *N.Y. Times*, Feb. 5, 1992, at A23 (supporting gay people's freedom to marry).

34. Steven K. Homer, Note, "Against Marriage," 29 *Harv. C.R.-C.L. L. Rev.* 505, 528 (1994).

35. Ruthann Robson, *Lesbian (Out)law* at 128 n. 12 (citing Joan Nestle, *A Restricted Country*, at 123, 1987).

36. See David W. Dunlap, "Some States Trying to Stop Gay Marriages Before They Start," *N.Y. Times*, Mar. 15, 1995, p. A18, col. 1

37. See "Recognition of Marriages," H.B. 366, Gen. Sess. (1995). See "Utah Won't Accept Same-Sex Marriages," *N.Y. Times*, Mar. 3, 1995; Tony Semarad, "Ban on Gay Marriages to be Annulled? Passage May Have Come Too Late to Be Valid," *Salt Lake Tribune*. See also Peter Freiberg, "Gays Win in South Dakota, Lose in Utah," *Wash. Blade*, Mar. 3, 1993, p. 1, col. 1.

38. Freiberg, *id.*

6

Being Raised in a Gay Family Does Not Harm Children

April Martin

April Martin, a clinical psychologist, is the executive vice president of the Gay and Lesbian Parents Coalition International and the author of The Lesbian and Gay Parenting Handbook.

Gays and lesbians make excellent parents because their children are planned for and truly wanted. Studies show that children raised by gay and lesbian parents are as emotionally and socially healthy as children of heterosexual parents. Children of homosexual parents usually have no problem adjusting to their different lifestyle, and they are often more tolerant and open-minded than other children.

Lesbian and gay parents are not a new phenomenon. There are an estimated 5 million to 6 million of them in this country, most of whom became parents in the context of a heterosexual marriage before they were fully aware of their sexual orientation. What is new, however, is that during the past two decades lesbians and gay men, perhaps tens of thousands, are choosing to become parents through adoption and artificial insemination. As the stigma evaporates and visibility increases, word is getting around among adoption, health care and child welfare professionals that families headed by lesbians and gays are working out successfully.

My own daughter will be 13 soon, and our son is almost 10. My life partner, a woman, and I began to plan this family 16 years ago. As we struggle to fit soccer practice, orthodontia appointments, music lessons, homework and family time into our schedules, we find it bewildering that anyone sees us as a threat to their values. We visit the grandparents, go to PTA meetings, attend church and have the occasional shopping spree. We hold strong ideas about what is important: education, ethics, responsibility, good manners—not exactly revolutionary fare.

Still, we live our lives against a backdrop of social prejudice. Antigay

From April Martin, "Gay-Parented Families Tout Traditional Values," *Insight*, July 25, 1994. Reprinted with permission of *Insight*. Copyright 1994 News World Communications, Inc. All rights reserved.

initiatives that threaten to create danger and suffering for our families are being proposed in many states. One proposal in Washington state would take children away from their lesbian or gay parents and place them in foster care—an astonishing cruelty in the name of family values.

Opposition to lesbian and gay families seems to come from two very different voices: the extremists of the Christian right, and a larger group of serious-minded people who aren't familiar with gay-parented families. There's not much we can say to the Christian far right, because they don't seem to be listening. They construct science-fiction horror stories to portray us as sexual abusers and "recruiters" of children. They cite bogus "research studies"—not compiled by reputable universities but by their own political organizations—to show that children with lesbian moms will grow up to be homosexual. They warn that gay parents will transmit AIDS to children, despite facts showing that children's HIV infections typically are acquired in the wombs of heterosexual mothers. They also ignore the fact that lesbians are in the lowest HIV group of the population and that gay men who are dealing with HIV generally are not the people seeking to become parents. They point to numerous studies showing that children of single mothers fare less well, ignoring the fact that lesbians in stable life-partnerships are not "single" in any but the strict legal sense and thus do not suffer the economic disadvantages which account for the plight of many single-parent families.

The Christian far right opposes school curricula that teach tolerance for diverse families, warning that children might get the idea that homosexuality is acceptable. They seem to assume that if heterosexual children were to see homosexuality as okay, nothing would stop them from rushing out and changing their sexual orientations. The vigorous crusaders dedicated to fighting lesbian- and gay-parented families clearly have more than reason invested in their position, and it is unlikely to be modified by exposure to the reality of who we are.

We lesbians and gay men choose to become parents for the same reasons heterosexuals do: to impart our love, our knowledge and our heritages to our children.

We very much want a dialogue, however, with those who bring unfamiliarity, rather than bigotry, to the issue. Their doubts about whether we can truly provide for the needs of children are precisely our concerns as well. We lesbians and gay men choose to become parents for the same reasons heterosexuals do: to impart our love, our knowledge and our heritages to our children and to experience the joy of helping a young heart and mind develop. Ultimately, we desire to fulfill some of what is best in humanity.

Not one of us would bring a child into our homes if we hadn't explored some hard questions: Can children grow up healthy with gay parents? What are their needs for role models of their own or the opposite gender? Are they likely to be harmed by prejudice? Will they have difficulties with friends or social life? Will they be confused about their own sexuality? These issues are vitally important to us.

Furthermore, judges, legislatures, educators and health care professionals also are asking the same questions. Gradually, they are familiarizing themselves with the research compiled during the last 15 years or so. What we know is based on approximately two dozen studies conducted by psychologists, psychiatrists and social workers. Most of the studies have compared the development of children raised by lesbian mothers or, in some cases, children raised by gay fathers with the development of children raised by heterosexual parents. According to Dr. Charlotte Patterson of the University of Virginia, writing in a 1992 issue of *Child Development* (considered the best journal in the field), a review of this research reveals that:

• Not a single study showed any difference in the children's level of emotional adjustment, whether raised by heterosexual or gay parents.

• Children raised by lesbian or gay parents were no more or less likely to be homosexual than other children.

• Boys showed no differences in tendency toward "masculine" behavior, mannerisms or interests, and girls showed no differences in "femininity."

• Despite the existence of social prejudice, children with lesbian or gay parents did just as well as other children socially and academically.

If myths about lesbians and gay men were true of us, I would agree that we shouldn't raise children. We are a highly diverse group, and though the media is fond of focusing on drag queens and motorcycle dykes, most of us less colorful folks have been invisible. This gradually is changing as more and more of us come out, giving our parents, extended families, neighbors and coworkers a chance to see us as real human beings.

Realities of gay parenting

Here are some of the realities:

Lesbians and gay men don't become parents accidentally. No one pressures them into parenthood. The ones who choose it are those with domestic enthusiasm and nurturing temperaments. Prospective parents often spend months and years in "considering parenthood" workshops to explore whether they realistically have the emotional, physical, financial, spiritual and community resources to be good parents. They discuss it with family, friends, clergy and psychotherapists. The children we adopt or conceive are among the most wanted and prepared for children on earth. Someday, perhaps, this standard will become the standard for all parents—even those who can create families without having to think about it.

Contrary to the Christian far right's portrayal of lesbians and gay men as sex-obsessed and depraved, our families are no more about sex than anyone else's. On an exhausting morning after I've stayed up late typing my daughter's science report, when there are school lunches to be packed and disputes to be settled about whose turn it is to play Nintendo, I could fall over laughing at the thought. We are an affectionate family—lots of hugging and kissing—but like most families, we believe that sexual activity is an extremely private matter. We respect our children's modesty and expect them to respect ours.

Lesbians do not hate men. Gay men do not hate women. We go out of our way to ensure that there are role models of the other gender in our children's lives. Along with other lesbian mothers, I am aware that my son needs someone with whom he can talk about "guy" things, and I want my children to grow up knowing and appreciating men. My kids have an adoring grandfather, and we have cultivated the children's relationships with some trusted male friends. (Unfortunately, many lesbians who conceive through artificial insemination are forced to use anonymous sperm donors, because laws fail to protect them from potentially devastating custody battles. If they had the same protection as families formed by adoption, they would be freer to use sperm donors whose identities are known to them and could more easily include biological fathers in their children's lives.)

It is love—not biology—that makes a family.

Lesbian and gay parents are prepared to accept their children's sexuality—whatever it may be. We assume that 90 to 95 percent of them will be heterosexual. We know from our own experience of being raised by heterosexual parents, in a heterosexual society, that sexual orientation is not subject to external dictates. We raise our children to be themselves.

And here's the part that surprised even many of us: It appears similarly impossible to influence gender-role behavior. I know some feminist lesbians who intended to raise daughters who could fix a car and wouldn't worry about hairdo and makeup. Lo and behold, they tell me, laughing, the universe sent them girls who want nail polish and Barbie dolls. They lovingly cave in, just as I have with a son who is wild for the goony machismo of the World Wrestling Federation. Values and character are things we can influence; preferences are to be discovered and accepted.

What makes our families different is not the nature of our parenting efforts, but the constellations of the families. The *Leave It to Beaver* model—one parent of each gender, both biologically related to the child, he the breadwinner, she the cookie baker—often is proffered as a societal standard, with worries that deviations may adversely affect children. In truth, this child-rearing arrangement is not the norm in many cultures and has never been as widespread in ours as the nostalgists would have us believe. Our experience, supported by child-development research and echoed by our kids themselves, shows that it is love—not biology—that makes a family. Our children have no trouble accepting what is common in many other societies—namely, that people who create you may not necessarily be the parents who raise you. Though they are given full and truthful information about their origins, their bonds are with those who are there to soothe a tummy ache, discuss a school problem or show them the wonders of a firefly.

But what about dealing with the larger world? Is it unfair to raise a child who may experience antigay bias because of his or her parents? Well, yes. It's as unfair as raising a female child in a sexist world or a child of color in a racist society. Prejudice is a tragic fact and one that I expect our children will make a contribution toward fighting when they grow up. Like other families who experience oppression, we try to give our children the tools to deal with it: self-esteem, social consciousness and courage.

In reality, however, the actual oppression they experience is far less than any of us would have imagined. My children have never been teased or harassed. They are popular and well-liked. The welcome we have found from our schools, neighborhood and friends has been heartwarming. I'm sure that if parents of their classmates had been polled before they knew us, many would have flatly disapproved of a two-mom family. Yet today their kids and ours share sleep-over dates, and we rely on each other for babysitting and mutual support. What's more, I've heard stories such as this from families all over the country, not just in liberal, urban areas. It sustains my faith that people will discard negative stereotypes that conflict with their face-to-face experience.

The issues at stake here are only partly about the rights of lesbians and gay men to parent and only partly about the legal and social rights of children in a variety of family structures. Also at stake are the rights of some children to have homes at all. Lesbians and gay men, who know the experience of being thrown away by society, frequently are willing to adopt children who are significantly physically and emotionally disabled. To deny lesbians and gay men the right to adopt, as do the states of New Hampshire and Florida and as many state legislatures are considering doing, is cruel and pointless. It condemns these children to institutional and foster care, at taxpayer expense, for no humane reason.

I share with families of any constellation a concern about the violence in our society; the failures of our educational systems; and the large numbers of young people damaged by drugs, alcohol, teenage pregnancy and lack of hope. It is my wish that we can work together to find solutions. As do many lesbian and gay parents, I teach my children tolerance for goodwilled people whose customs, characteristics or beliefs differ from mine. It is hard to see how teaching tolerance for our families and granting them basic legal protections does any harm to those who live differently—even to the unfortunate minority who teach their children to fear and hate.

7

Same-Sex Marriage Ceremonies Affirm Gay Love

John J. McNeill

John J. McNeill is an ordained Roman Catholic priest and a practicing psychotherapist. His refusal to stop ministering to gay men and lesbians resulted in his expulsion from the Society of Jesus in 1987. He is the author of The Church and the Homosexual, Taking a Chance on God, *and* Freedom, Glorious Freedom: The Spiritual Journey to the Fullness of Life for Gays, Lesbians, and Everybody Else.

The need for human companionship can be fulfilled in a gay relationship as well as in a heterosexual one. The Christian church has a long history of sanctioning same-sex marriages. These ancient ceremonies—the same ones used to bless heterosexual marriages—allowed gay couples to affirm their love for each other. If same-sex marriage ceremonies were more widely accepted, more gay couples would be able to openly celebrate their union, and heterosexual society would realize that gays are capable of sincere, committed relationships.

When I published *The Church and the Homosexual,* one of the chapters Church censors demanded I suppress in order to receive the *imprimi potest,* the official approval to publish, was the chapter on gay marriages. At this time, rather than gay marriage or gay union, I prefer to use the term lesbian or gay covenanted union. I prefer this terminology because marriage is derived from a French root referring to husband, *mari,* and "union" speaks only of the fusion of two partners. It can be understood as one losing his or her identity and assuming the identity of the other person, as it traditionally did in heterosexual unions, complete to the woman's losing her name. Rather than view the relationship as some kind of complete merging or blending as "union" alone might suggest, the term "covenanted union" encourages us to see a give-and-receive relationship that seeks, with the help of God, the fulfillment of two individuals. It is a "meeting of souls, souls which although eternally separate, can grow into harmony such as no other human relationship can make possible."[1]

It is with great joy that I now have the freedom publicly to record and celebrate this rite as one of the most powerful witnesses to the goodness and the holiness of gay love. During the past year I had the privilege of being invited to preside at two covenanted unions; the first was for two gay friends in the metropolitan New York area and the second was for two lesbian friends in upstate New York. In both cases all the parties involved had done a remarkably good job of making the first two passages of self-acceptance and coming out to others. I also had the privilege of being present in Pullam Baptist Church in Raleigh, North Carolina, when that church chose to celebrate a covenanted union of two gay men in the sanctuary. What was surprising and hopeful about that event was that, after long and public debate, three-quarters of the church's straight congregation approved the ceremony. In every instance, these covenantal unions were occasions of deep spiritual blessings and great peace and joy. They were transformative not only for the couple involved but for the whole community of family and friends that took part in the ritual.

God is just as much present and involved in a loving gay Christian relationship as God is in a straight one.

I have a firm conviction that God is just as much present and involved in a loving gay Christian relationship as God is in a straight one. Genesis (2:18) tells us: "It is not good that a human remain alone. Every human has need of a companion of his or her own kind!"[2] This divine purpose of companionship can be fulfilled in a gay relationship just as well as in a straight one. In fact, some people would argue that the equality that is more often recognized between gay partners makes them more capable of fulfilling that function.

From the moment the Catholic Church granted the morality of the rhythm method as a natural form of birth control for straight couples and justified sexual activity as still fulfilling what Vatican II referred to as "the equally primary aims of mutual love and fulfillment," there was a serious reason to reconsider the position that all homosexual activities are necessarily wrong on the ground that they cannot lead to procreation. In a passage in the Papal encyclical *Casti Connubii,* the mutual love between the partners is recognized in its own right as the "primary purpose and meaning of matrimony."

> The mutual inward molding of the partners, this determined effort to perfect each other, can in a very real sense . . . be said to be the chief reason and purpose of matrimony, provided matrimony be looked at not in the restricted sense as instituted for the proper conception and education of children, but more widely as the blending of life as a whole and the mutual interchange and sharing thereof.[3]

As Daniel Maguire, a noted Christian ethicist, pointed out in his article "The Morality of Homosexual Marriage," "Erotic desire is deeply interwoven into the human desire and need for closeness and for trusting relationships. The desire for a significant other with whom we are uniquely conjoined is not a heterosexual but a basic human desire. The programmatic exclusion of gay persons from the multiple benefits of erotic attraction, which often opens the way to such a union, is arbitrary, harmful, cruel, and therefore sinful."[4]

An ancient tradition

Gay and lesbian Christians should be aware that in requesting the right to a rite of covenantal union in the Church, we are only reclaiming what is an ancient tradition in the Church. John Boswell has done extensive research on the history of gay ceremonies of covenanted union and has found hundreds of lectionary services for holy unions or marriages for gay persons in ancient Church documents going back as far as the third century. Boswell traces a fifteen-hundred-year period in Church history in which the Church blessed lesbian and gay relationships. My favorite was a special blessed bonding of Irish warriors before they went into combat together.

Boswell points out that heterosexual marriages were not considered sacramental unions until as late as the thirteenth century. Most straight marriages were seen as a civil contract in which one bought a wife. "Romantic love had never been a part of the Catholic heterosexual tradition. Up until the 11th century people would not have thought of looking for love in marriage. . . . Marriage was based on respect, on procreation and on family alliance."[5]

Boswell traces the origins of the first church-sponsored heterosexual wedding ceremonies which celebrate romantic love between the partners as having been borrowed from the gay ceremonies for the making of "spiritual brotherhood" between two men; terms that Boswell points out should not be taken to mean nonromantic or necessarily nonsexual.

By the power of the [marriage] ritual the couple become united emotionally not only with each other but with the community as well.

In most of these ceremonies there was a retelling from the *Acts of the Martyrs* of the martyrdom of Bacchus and Serge. They were soldiers in the Roman army in the late third or early fourth century, very highly placed, great favorites of the pagan Roman emperor. They are called in their official Greek biography "erosti" which means gay lovers. They were denounced to the emperor for being Christian, so he asked them, as a sign of their loyalty to him, to sacrifice to pagan gods. They refused to do that. They said that they were loyal servants, but that their loyalty did not involve denying the one true God. The emperor went into a rage and ordered their belts cut off, their tunics and all other military garb removed, the gold torques taken from around their necks, and women's clothing placed on them.

To disgrace them, the emperor ordered them to be paraded through the middle of Rome to the palace wearing women's clothing and heavy chains. As they were paraded through the city, instead of feeling disgrace, they chanted together: "Yea, though we walk through the valley of the shadow of death, we will fear no evil, Lord, because denying ungodliness and worldly lusts, we have put off the form of the old man and we rejoice in you naked because you have clothed us with the garment of salvation; you have covered us with the robe of righteousness; and you have decked us as brides with women's gowns and joined us together one to the other for you through our faithfulness."[6]

Serge and Bacchus were then subjected to horrible tortures. Bacchus finally died and Serge wavered in his faith, weeping and crying out: "Oh, my other half, never again will we sing together the psalms we used to sing. Unyoked from me you have gone to heaven and left me alone here on earth, lonely and disconsolate." Then Bacchus appeared to Serge radiantly beautiful and said: "Why do you mourn and grieve, beloved? I have been taken from you bodily, but in the bond of our love I am with you still. Hurry now, so that through good and perfect fidelity you may be worthy to earn me as the reward of the race, for my crown of justice is you."

The first time I read this account, shivers ran down my spine. In the monasteries and convents of old, two gay men or two lesbian women would read this account and believe that their love for each other was a good and holy human love that would exist not only in this world, but would actually continue to exist for all eternity in the next. It was this concept of the basis for marriage as the genuine love between two humans as equal that gradually led to the heterosexual sacrament of marriage. The very formulas for gay and lesbian unions were the ones first used in church marriages of heterosexuals.

The importance of a ceremony

Why have a public Christian ceremony? Usually the individuals involved are looking for at least three things: affirmation, celebration, and symbolization of their relationship. The primary reason for a Christian ceremony as such should be your faith in the God which Christian tradition professes. "Whoever fails to love does not know God, because God is love!" (1 John 4:7–8). At the heart of a Christian ceremony of covenanted union is the self-giving of each mate to God, an invitation and openness to and declaration of God's loving presence in each of their lives. It is a making and preserving of a relationship of trust with this God who is the source of your love and who helps you to discover the divine course of your relationship. A wonderful attribute of a Christian ceremony is that it allows the gay couple to experience, to feel, and to know that they are within the full bonds of God's grace.

The ceremony allows the couple to declare to the world their love for each other and invite the world to come and see their shared love. In so doing, the couple strengthen each other, build each other up with an unabashed declaration of love. It can also produce a new spiritual awareness and a new understanding of who they are as a couple.

Not only do you affirm your love for each other in the act of a public ceremony, but you, along with the witnesses, also send out a message to society that what you are doing is right and just. It allows you to see, also, that others are invested in your relationship. As you become bonded in the eyes of a community which you hold dear, those of your friends and family, any discussion of a breakup will carry with it a heightened awareness of the gravity of the separation. By the power of the ritual the couple become united emotionally not only with each other but with the community as well. This can provide the foundation to see the couple through difficult times and provide "landmarks of remembrance and hope" during times of crisis.

If more gays and lesbians were to celebrate their unions, our society would awaken to the fact that sincere, committed relationships are not foreign to the gay community.

If more gays and lesbians were to celebrate their unions, our society would awaken to the fact that sincere, committed relationships are not foreign to the gay community, but are, instead, rather common. As more people witness our ceremonies, society would begin to realize that the level of integrity in gay relationships is no less than that in straight relationships. Lawmakers might begin to understand that their refusal to recognize our relationships legally is completely unjust. Our ceremonies could fight the prejudice which maintains that we, as gay people, do not merit the rights afforded to nongay couples because we do not take our relationships seriously. We do not live isolated lives; our lives happen in the context of community. Our ceremonies help to insure that our community is more than just merely accommodating, but truly affirming and supportive.

Evelyn and James Whitehead make the interesting observation that the Christian Church as an institution is also in a process of gradually "coming out."[7] That coming out process is at various stages of maturity in different denominations. We have seen over the past year many denominations publicly debating the feasibility of ordaining gay clergy in an open relationship. Many churches have adopted open door policies for gays and lesbians, accepting them as equal members of the congregation. Many dioceses of the American Catholic Church have made sensitive pastoral moves, acknowledging their gay members. Many have established special "task forces" concerned with ministry to lesbian and gay Catholics. In acknowledging the existence of and then creating public space for homosexual Catholics to stand in the community, the Church facilitates this third, public passage. As the Whiteheads observe, in doing this the Church senses, though not without some anxiety and self-doubt, that it is these maturing lesbian and gay Christians who will witness to believers the shape of homosexual holiness. However, for every positive step the American Church takes in its pastoral sensitivity to the needs of gay Catholics, the latest missive from Rome seems to send the American Church reeling backward two steps. Despite this opposition recent surveys show that over 84 percent of lay Catholics support gay rights and a greater acceptance of gay members on the part of the Church.

This is a wonderful time to be gay and Christian! How many of our gay ancestors who lived necessarily closeted, secretive lives would have rejoiced to have had one iota of the freedom we have to live out of the closet, to come together as Christians in worship and prayer, to be able to live openly in a gay relationship? My heart is continually filled with joyful gratitude to God for this blessing both for myself and my partner, Charlie, and for all my gay brothers and sisters.

Notes

1. Kenneth Forman, *From This Day Forward* (Richmond, Va.: Outlook Publishers, 1950), p. 10. I wish to acknowledge my debt of gratitude to Sean Murray for sharing with me his unpublished manuscript, "In Front of God and Everybody: A Gay Man's Guide to Ceremonies of Covenantal Union," 1 April 1992.

2. A direct translation from the Hebrew by Phyllis Trible, Professor of Old Testament Studies, Union Theological Seminary, New York, New York.

3. Pope Pius XI, *Casti Connubii, The Church and the Reconstruction of the Modern World*, The Social Encyclicals of Pius XI, ed. Terence P. McLaughlin (Garden City, NY: Doubleday, 1957), p. 59. The same point is made strongly in the "Pastoral Constitution on the Church in the Modern World," *Documents of Vatican II*, pp. 314–15: "Therefore, marriage persists as a whole manner and communion of life, and maintains its value and indissolubility, even when offspring are lacking—despite, rather often, the very intense desire of the couple." No. 50.

4. Daniel Maguire, "The Morality of Homosexual Marriage," in *A Challenge to Love: Gay and Lesbian Catholics in the Church*, ed. Robert Nugent (New York: Crossroad. 1983). p. 120.

5. John Boswell, *Same-Sex Unions in Pre-Modern Europe*. This manuscript is expected to be published in the spring of 1994.

6. Ibid.

7. Evelyn and James Whitehead, *Seasons of Strength: New Visions of Adult Christian Maturing* (Garden City, NY: Image Books/Doubleday, 1986), p. 186.

8

Same-Sex Marriage Would Save Society Money

Ann Rostow

Ann Rostow is a staff writer for the San Francisco Bay Times, *a newspaper for gays and lesbians.*

Claims that same-sex marriages would cost the government money are false. Same-sex marriages would actually save taxpayer dollars because they would lessen the state's responsibility for the health and welfare of many indigent gay and lesbian citizens. Marriage would not result in economic gains for gays and lesbians. However, gays are fighting for the right of same-sex marriage not because it would lead to profit, but because it would provide them with economic security.

Numbers are like Bible passages. If you quote them out of context, you can prove any point you like.

California Representative Pete Knight (R-Palmdale), the sponsor of two anti-marriage bills, issued a statement in 1995 summarizing the costs to the state of recognizing same-sex marriage. Presented in brief bullets on a page, Knight's list appears to add up to thousands of dollars per couple per year in new costs to society, or what he calls "economic marriage benefits subsidized by taxpayers and business owners." As his source for the figures, Knight cites the Hawaii Commission on Sexual Orientation and the Law, the legislative task force which in 1995 recommended that the state of Hawaii legalize same-sex marriage or at least initiate far-reaching domestic partnership rules to balance the scales between gay and straight relationships.

We can thank Mr. Knight for telling us where he got his figures, since a look at the original testimony completely repudiates Knight's conclusions. And while an article on competitive number-crunching may not seem like the most interesting aspect of the fight for same-sex marriage, it's a worthwhile exercise. As opponents of same-sex marriage attempt to turn economics into a "mainstream" argument to back their viewpoints,

From Ann Rostow, "The Numbers Game: Why Same-Sex Marriage Saves Money," *San Francisco Bay Times*, March 21, 1995. Reprinted with permission.

it's important for supporters to know why same-sex marriage—if anything—will *save* taxpayer dollars.

The "cost" of simulating marriage

The most expensive "marriage benefit" on Knight's list is a one-time figure of $6,800 which represents "documenting of legal relationship between couples automatically provided by government in first year of marriage."

What does this mean?

Knight's original source material is the testimony of Sumner La Croix, a professor of economics at the University of Hawaii, summarized in the commission report by La Croix and Lee Badgett, a professor of public affairs at the University of Maryland. Knight's $6,800 "documentation cost" is in fact an estimate of what it would cost in theory to assemble the legal documents that a marriage automatically represents.

La Croix and Badgett testified that "in one relatively simple step, marriage creates a relationship between two adults that grants several rights that can otherwise be simulated with private agreements between two unmarried partners." Among the contracts implicitly contained in marriage, the professors went on to list access to family court, defined principles for the dissolution of the relationship, inheritance rights included in the probate code and others.

Setting up special contracts to cover various aspects of a relationship in the absence of marriage is complicated. "These documents often require the costly services of a lawyer," the testimony explained. "Marriage allows a couple to save the money and time costs associated with drawing up these documents. These economic benefits can be significant, amounting to several thousand dollars."

So let's dismiss Mr. Knight's first "cost to taxpayers and business owners." The government itself does not incur any expense, let alone an expense of $6,800, for recognizing a marriage. Perhaps if one considers lawyers in the category of "business owners," some gay and lesbian lawyers will lose potential income from couples who—without marriage—would have chosen to set up their own intricate legal arrangements.

Taxes

The next largest item on Knight's list is $4,500 simply listed as annual "Income Tax Benefits."

Without getting into an unwieldy analysis of the federal tax code, the general pattern rewards couples in which one partner works and the other does not, and penalizes couples in which both partners work and earn similar incomes. In California's state tax code, the marriage penalty has been eliminated, but the bulk of income taxes are paid to the IRS, not the Franchise Tax Board. In their section on the impact of marriage on taxes, Professors La Croix and Badgett reviewed several scenarios. In some, the couple's taxes increased, and in others, the couple's taxes decreased.

Clearly Pete Knight's "income tax benefit" may well apply to some relationships, but many others will pay the famous "marriage penalty." As for the actual figure of $4,500 in tax savings, it would apply in the specific case of a (very rich) couple who not only benefit from marriage under the tax code, but who also earn a figure high enough to account for $4,500 in such benefits.

Health benefits

The next cost to society according to Knight is an annual $1,251 in health benefits presumably paid by the employer of a working spouse to the unemployed partner.

There are three quick points to raise on this issue. First of all, in couples where both partners are already employed and insured, the partners will either keep their current policies, or—if they decide to switch one policy to a spousal benefit, they will cancel the other coverage. There are no net added insurance costs to employers in these cases.

Second, in the case of a couple in which one partner is employed and the other partner is unemployed *and uninsured*, the taxpayers are presently paying the medical bills for the uninsured partner. He or she, as an unmarried person, is probably qualifying for government assistance and/or using emergency public medical facilities. Note that if their marriage is legally recognized, the income of the employed partner lifts the other person out of the hard-luck range of all government programs. The spouse becomes the safety net and the cost to society substantially *decreases*.

Same-sex marriage—if anything—will save *taxpayer dollars.*

Lastly, let's refer back to the original testimony from which Knight drew his figure: "If the spouse is not working," said the professors, "then the spouse can be enrolled in, for example, the HGEA's [Hawaii Government Employees' Association] 'Kaiser Gold' package. . . . If the alternative is an individual health care policy from Kaiser, then the annual benefit from including the spouse in the employee's health care plan is $1,251.48."

Professors La Croix and Badgett have offered the *example* of the HGEA "Kaiser Gold" package, whatever that may entail, and compared it with the actual out-of-pocket costs of an individual Kaiser policy in order to evaluate the worth of the benefit to a couple. The state of Hawaii is not paying $1,251.48! The state is adding one person to a huge pool of a negotiated state insurance program at a fraction of that cost.

Knight has taken the price tag off this illustration and turned it into a statement of numerical fact under the heading "Subsidized health insurance for spouse."

The safety net

Unfortunately for readers, there is more. Knight has lifted the figure of $1,872 per year as the cost of "Additional social security disability payments to spouses of disabled workers."

Where to begin.

In terms of the government safety net programs, recognizing same-sex marriage will save society money. In his example, Knight has cherry-picked an illustration describing a spousal benefit, and ignored the fact that a qualification for SSI [Supplemental Security Income], Medicare and so forth takes into account the joint assets of a legally married couple. If an unmarried lesbian mom has three kids and a multimillionaire lover, she may still qualify for Aid to Families with Dependent Children [AFDC], even if she drives a Mercedes to pick up her check. But if she is allowed to marry her lover, the lover takes over the bills. (Anyone who listened to the stump speeches of 1996 GOP presidential candidate Lamar Alexander heard about the dilemma of a "couple I met down in Nashua," who went over to the welfare office and were advised to separate in order to increase their welfare benefits.)

Recognizing same-sex marriages is not just the right thing to do, it's the economically conservative thing to do as well.

But of course some gay and lesbian couples will have a combined income below the poverty line and will qualify for government aid under Knight's example. So let's read the commission testimony which produced his quote of $1,872 per year:

"If a disabled worker has a spouse who is either aged 62 or older or is caring for a young or disabled child of the worker, the spouse is eligible for a benefit that averaged $156 per month or $1,872 annually in 1993."

No one, with the possible exception of Knight, would argue that a financially strapped couple, where one partner is disabled and the other is either aging or taking care of children with no money, should not be eligible for some kind of assistance. If such a couple is considered married, they may apply for the SSI program described above. If not, they may apply as individuals for assistance through other programs. The fact is, if both members of the couple are broke, they are eligible for some kind of welfare whether their marriage is recognized or not. However, when one partner has an income, recognizing marriage will lift the other partner out of eligibility.

Retirement expense

We are not quite finished with Knight's list. Under the category of retirement benefits, he has included $1,461 per year for the spouses of public employees, $553 per year in subsidized Medicare premium for spouse, and $4,164 in "50% additional benefits for the spouse of retired worker full insured under OASI (Old Age and Survivors Inheritance)."

Knight picked up the first two figures from an estimate of health insurance benefits provided by the State of Hawaii's Employee Retirement System. After retirement, a Hawaii government employee gets continuing health insurance as does the employee's spouse "if he/she is neither covered at work nor by another retirement plan." Likewise, the same plan will pay half the Medicare "Part B" program for a spouse if the spouse has no other coverage.

The first problem is that these numbers refer to a specific plan for retired employees of the state of Hawaii, not to gay and lesbian couples in California—but let's give Knight the benefit of the doubt by assuming that the state of California has some similar program, and that gays and lesbians working for the state will retire and want such benefits for their spouses.

As with the case of corporate health plans, net extra benefits come into play when the spouse has no other source of coverage. We are therefore talking about a couple in which one person has presumably worked hard for the state of California and earned a pension, while the other partner has reached retirement age without health insurance.

If these two are not considered married, who do you think picks up the medical bills for the uninsured partner? Fortunately, we do not yet live in a society where an elderly person with no money is left to die in medical crisis, so some government program—presumably MediCal—will kick in with funding.

The same phenomenon is true in the case of Old Age and Survivors Insurance, a social security program that covers the spouses of retired workers who die. Again, by using OASI as an example Knight is by definition referring to a situation in which one member of the partnership has been employed and the other has not, exactly the type of couple that will dramatically save money for the state should their marriage be legalized.

Married couples save taxpayer money, period

Lee Badgett, who is preparing a Briefing Paper on the state-by-state economic impact of same-sex marriage for the Institute of Gay and Lesbian Strategic Studies in Washington, D.C., points out that in California, 65 percent of single-parent family households receive AFDC, while 3 percent of two-parent married couples qualify under much stricter standards. In 1993, the average yearly cost to the state and federal government for a family on AFDC in California was $6,235.

The average cost of MediCal per AFDC recipient in 1992 was $1,480 per year and $652 per child, again shared equally by the state and federal government.

Every 100 families leaving the AFDC program save taxpayers a million dollars a year.

As for the extension of health insurance, whether through a company or through a pension program, Badgett repeats the point that health insurance is cheaper to society as a whole. "Recognizing marriages of the currently uninsured might mean some small increase in employers' costs," she writes, "but would likely mean reducing the amount of uncompensated care that is a growing burden on health care providers, private insurers and the state." Knight simply can't have it both ways.

The real benefits of marriage

After all of this, some people might be asking why we're fighting so hard for the "benefits" of marriage if they include higher taxes, loss of eligibility for government aid, financial responsibility under the law for our partners' kids, etc.

In fact, gays and lesbians are not fighting for the right to marry in order to improve their family finances, and never have been. The chief economic benefits of marriage are those of security, not gain. Marriage secures parental rights, inheritance rights, and allows a couple to live and plan jointly without the fear that if one of them dies, their house and savings could be awarded to a remote cousin rather than a surviving spouse. Gay and lesbian couples fortunate enough to pay a marriage penalty on their taxes will gladly do so in return for the knowledge that their children are part of a legally recognized two-parent family. And many gay and lesbian couples will be happy to trade one member's MediCal eligibility for a spousal health insurance policy.

Marriage is a complicated institution, so there will be some situations where new marriages appear to "cost" the community. But while Pete Knight can throw around handfuls of unsupported numbers out of context as much as he likes, any serious legislator who bases his or her vote on fiscal factors will have no choice but to vote against anti-marriage bills. Recognizing same-sex marriages is not just the right thing to do, it's the economically conservative thing to do as well.

9

Same-Sex Marriage Should Not Be Legal

Robert H. Knight

Robert H. Knight is the director of cultural studies at the Family Research Council, a research and educational organization in Washington, D.C., that promotes traditional family values. Knight wrote the following viewpoint in a question-and-answer format.

Marriage as traditionally defined—the union of one man and one woman—is the most important social institution around the world. Legalizing same-sex marriage would turn the state against those who believe in the traditional definition of marriage. Furthermore, eliminating the prohibition of gay marriage could lead to the removal of other restrictions, such as age requirements or the ban against polygamous marriages. A tiny minority of the population should not be allowed to change society's moral codes.

Q: In restricting marriage to one man and one woman, aren't you imposing your beliefs on others?

A: Marriage has been the foundation of civilization for thousands of years in cultures around the world. It is the single most important social institution, and it is the basis for the procreation of children and the heart of family life. Those who are trying to radically redefine it for their own purposes are the ones who are trying to impose their values on the rest of the population. Ordinary people did not pick this fight. They are not the aggressors. They are merely defending the basic morality that has sustained the culture for everyone against a radical attack.

The effects of same-sex marriage

Q: Oh, come on. Whom does it really hurt if a same-sex couple want to get married?

A: When homosexual couples seek state approval and all the benefits that the state reserves for married couples, they impose the law on every-

From Robert H. Knight, "Answers to Questions About the Defense of Marriage," *Pro and Con*, March 22, 1996, at http://www.nonline.com/procon/html/gaymarcon.html. Reprinted with permission from the author.

one. According non-marital relationships the same status as marriage would mean that millions of people would be disenfranchised by their own governments. The state would be telling them that their beliefs are no longer valid, and would turn the civil rights laws into a battering ram against them:

- Business men and women would be required to provide "family" health benefits to homosexual couples.
- Children would be taught in schools that homosexual sex is the moral equivalent of marital love.
- Same-sex "marriage" would facilitate the adoption of children by homosexual couples.
- Sex-based distinctions in the law would be removed (as was proposed in the rejected Equal Rights Amendment).

Law is not a suggestion, but, as George Washington observed, it is force. Official state sanction of same-sex relationships as "marriage" would bring the full apparatus of the state against those who believe that marriage is between one man and one woman. Traditional morality would, in effect, be outlawed.

Q: But if two people—any two people—love each other, why not let them marry?

A: Marriage is not just a matter of feelings. It is the specifically defined legal, social, economic and spiritual union of a man and a woman. The two sexes must be present for it to be marriage. If that definition is radically altered based on the "feelings" of those in other relationships, then the sky is the limit. There is no logical reason for not letting several people marry, or for gutting other requirements, such as minimum age, blood relative status or even the limitation of the relationship to human beings.

Marriage is not just a matter of feelings. It is the specifically defined legal, social, economic and spiritual union of a man and a woman.

Q: Don't morals change? Haven't we heard all these tired phrases used in defense of not letting women vote or even in defense of slavery?

A: Various social movements have succeeded because they were in accord with natural law and the basic precepts of the moral code. Homosexuality has never been considered morally good, and it is a quantum leap from ending slavery to saying that homosexuality must now be considered good, healthy and worthy of state-protected benefits. Homosexuals enjoy all the rights every other citizen already has—they can vote, own property, etc.—but they cannot claim special treatment beyond those rights. Anytime they achieve that, they threaten the civil rights of those who disagree with them.

Q: For years, in some Southern states, blacks and whites were prevented from marrying by anti-miscegenation laws. Eventually, the courts overturned these laws. Aren't same-sex couples being similarly discriminated against? Isn't it only a matter of time before these repressive laws are also overturned?

A: As Colin Powell has observed, skin color and sexual behavior are entirely different. The first is a benign, inborn characteristic that has no bearing on conduct or character; the second is behaviorally based and has everything to do with character, morality and society's basic rules of conduct. If the civil rights laws begin deviating into behavior and away from race, ethnic origin, place of birth or other immutable characteristics, there is no stopping point. New laws would have to be coined almost daily to accommodate the flood of claims based on behavior (smokers, compulsive gamblers, pornography fanatics, sex addicts and pedophiles could all claim new "rights" to protection against discrimination). One non-immutable characteristic that does get protection is religion, because that is enshrined in the Constitution. But there is no constitutional right to engage in sodomy (see *Bowers v. Hardwick*)[1] and demand that the state elevate it into protected status.

Q: But studies show that homosexuals are born that way. How then can you blame them for their condition?

A: Nobody is "blaming" anyone for having homosexual desires. The "genetic" studies that have been publicized have been conducted by self-styled homosexual activists or have been misrepresented in the media. The studies themselves typically have tiny sample sizes, biased selection, and other major methodological flaws, and are not replicated by reputable scientists.[2] By contrast, 70 years of therapeutic counseling and case studies show a remarkable consistency concerning the origins of the homosexual impulse as an uncompleted gender identity seeking after its own sex to replace what was not fully developed.[3] Do homosexuals choose to be gay? Mostly, no, but they can choose their behavior, and they can change their orientation,[4] as researchers Masters and Johnson showed in their landmark studies[5] and as numerous examples of successful personal transformation testify.[6]

Marriage is the bringing together of the two sexes.
That is the whole point.

Q: Isn't the traditional view of marriage religious in nature? And if so, doesn't the restriction of marriage to one man and one woman violate the religious beliefs of those who disagree?

A: Although marriage does indeed arise from religious traditions, most notably the Bible, it is an independently quantifiable good for society. Hence, the state has an interest in preserving and protecting the special status of marriage, regardless of religious beliefs. A society can get along just fine without any homosexuality, but no society can get along without marriage. That is why the state encourages marriage. In 1885, the Supreme Court felt so strongly that marriage was to be protected that it declared it as a requirement for admission of new states to the Union. Any prospective state, the court said, had to have law resting "on the basis of the idea of the family, as consisting in and springing from the union for life of one man and one woman in the holy estate of matrimony; the sure foundation of all that is stable and noble in our civilization, the best guaranty of that reverent morality which is the source of all beneficent progress in social and political improvement."[7]

Q: What about childless couples? Since you say that marriage must be protected partly because of its importance in forming families, does this mean that heterosexual couples who do not have children shouldn't get marriage licenses?

A: Of course not. Although most people marry with the intention of someday starting families, the married couples who do not have children still have the potential for becoming mothers and fathers, either biologically or through adoption. Marriage is a societal good even without children, as husbands and wives serve as role models for children in their neighborhoods. Procreation is an important aspect of society's high regard for marriage, but it is not the only reason marriage is protected. Children do not benefit when homosexuality is presented as a neutral or positive lifestyle choice.

Homosexual monogamy is a fiction

Q: But with the threat of AIDS and other diseases among promiscuous, homosexual men, wouldn't it be a societal good to encourage homosexual monogamy?

A: In cities where homosexual monogamy is already being encouraged, AIDS and other sexually transmitted diseases are skyrocketing.[8] It is not "homophobia" that is causing this, but the behavior itself, which is destructive emotionally, physically and morally to individuals, families and societies. That is why it has been discouraged in all successful cultures. Socrates and Plato wrote that homosexuality was harmful to individuals and society and should be discouraged. Even in "steady" homosexual relationships, dangerous sex occurs, since the defining homosexual sex act is patently unhealthy by any standard. State sanction of homosexuality in any form is an invitation to the young to experiment with something that may prove deadly. Any public health benefits available by discouraging promiscuous homosexual activity can be achieved without redefining traditional marriage, which is per se a profoundly important public health measure.

Besides, homosexual literature acknowledges that homosexual "monogamy" is largely fictional. Most homosexual relationships are fleeting. Those that endure more than a few years do so because of an agreement to have outside partners. As former *New Republic* editor Andrew Sullivan, a homosexual, writes in his book *Virtually Normal*, "the openness of the contract" of homosexual "marriage" reflects "greater understanding of the need for extramarital outlets between two men than between a man and a woman." In other words, the homosexual concept of "monogamy" is non-monogamous. Homosexual activist Michelangelo Signorile frankly admits that the goal of homosexual activists is to "fight for same-sex marriage and its benefits and then, once granted, redefine the institution of marriage completely, to demand the right to marry not as a way of adhering to society's moral codes but rather to debunk a myth and radically alter an archaic institution. . . ."[9]

Q: Don't most people want homosexuals to be treated fairly?

A: Yes. Most people have no ill will toward homosexuals, but this does not mean that a tiny segment of the population (less than 2 percent) should be allowed to radically redefine society's moral code. Even in liberal Hawaii, recent polls show that more than 70 percent of residents oppose same-sex "marriage," and national polls show that about two-thirds of respondents oppose same-sex "marriage." This is not about tolerance, but about a tiny group seeking to use the law to impose its version of morality on everyone else.

Q: Still, don't homosexuals suffer discrimination when they can't marry?

A: No. Homosexuals have precisely the same right to marry as anyone else. Marriage is the bringing together of the two sexes. That is the whole point. To enter marriage, you must meet its qualifications. Any attempt to get around the rules that everyone else plays by is an attempt to have special rights, not equal rights. Eliminating an entire sex from the picture and then calling it "marriage" is not a mere expansion of an institution, but rather the destruction of a principle.

Q: What about domestic partnerships? If you won't go along with same-sex "marriage," why not at least allow committed same-sex couples to get some benefits?

A: The state should never be in the business of encouraging unhealthy behavior by granting special benefits for it. A homosexual life does not offer the richness of the complementary relationship that men and women find in marriage and family life. People should not be written off as if they can do no better than be mired in an unhealthy, unnatural behavior. The more that homosexuality is encouraged, the more damage will be wreaked among individuals, families and society. This is not compassion but its opposite: a ruthless social Darwinism that devalues people as impulse-driven incorrigibles. Each human soul is of inestimable worth, and homosexuals are no different from anyone else. They deserve the truth, not an officially sanctioned lie.

Notes

1. *Bowers v. Hardwick* 478 U.S. 186, 190 (1986). In rejecting the claim, the Court said, "Nor are we inclined to take a more expansive view of our authority to discover new fundamental rights imbedded in the Due Process Clause. The Court is most vulnerable and comes nearest to illegitimacy when it deals with judge-made constitutional law having little or no cognizable roots in the language or design of the Constitution. . . . There should be, therefore, great resistance to expand the substantive reach of those Clauses, particularly if it requires redefining the category of rights deemed to be fundamental."

2. See, for instance, William Byne and Bruce Parsons, "Human Sexual Orientation: The Biological Theories Reappraised," *Archives of General Psychiatry*, Vol. 50, March 1993, pp. 228–239.

3. See Elizabeth R. Moberly, *Psychogenesis: The Early Development of Gender Identity* (London: Routledge & Kegan Paul Limited, 1983); Joseph Nicolosi, Ph.D., *Reparative Therapy of Male Homosexuality* (Northvale, New Jersey: Jason Aronson Inc., 1991); and Charles W. Socarides, M.D., *Homosexuality: A Freedom Too Far* (Phoenix: Adam Margrave Books, 1995).

4. E. Mansell Pattison, M.D., and Myrna Loy Pattison, "Ex-Gays: Religiously Mediated Change in Homosexuals," *American Journal of Psychiatry*, 137: 12, December 1980. "All subjects manifested major before-after changes.

Corollary evidence suggests that the phenomenon of substantiated change in sexual orientation without explicit treatment and/or long-term psychotherapy may be much more common than previously thought." (P. 1553.)

5. Mark F. Schwartz and William H. Masters, "The Masters and Johnson Treatment Program for Dissatisfied Homosexual Men," *American Journal of Psychiatry*, 141, 1984, pp. 173–181.

6. For example, Starla Allen, "Uncovering the Real Me," *Exodus International Update*, February 1996; Richard A. Cohen, M.A., "TCM Testimony of the Month," *Transformation Press*, No. 19, February 1996, p. 3.

7. *Murphy v. Ramsey* 114 U.S. 15, 45 (1885).

8. Survey from the Centers for Disease Control reported by Associated Press, "HIV Found in 7 Percent of Gay Young Men: Education Fails to Halt Spread," *Washington Times*, February 11, 1996, p. A-3; Michael Warner, "Why Gay Men Are Having Risky Sex," *Village Voice*, New York, January 31, 1995, Vol. XL, No. 5.

9. Quoted in *Out* magazine, December/January 1994, p. 161.

10

Prohibiting Same-Sex Marriage Is Constitutional

Michael W. McConnell

Michael W. McConnell is the William B. Graham Professor at the University of Chicago Law School.

The Full Faith and Credit Clause of the U.S. Constitution requires that all states recognize the laws and legal judgments of other states, including marriages and divorces. However, the clause also gives Congress the power to dictate how one state's laws shall affect another state's laws. Therefore, this clause gives Congress the authority to legislate that a same-sex marriage performed in one state need not be recognized in other states.

Editor's note: The following viewpoint is a letter written July 10, 1996, to Orrin G. Hatch, the chairman of the Senate Committee on the Judiciary, concerning the Defense of Marriage Act. The act, signed into law by Bill Clinton in September 1996, defines marriage as "a legal union between one man and one woman as husband and wife."

Dear Mr. Chairman: I am writing in response to arguments that the proposed Defense of Marriage Act is beyond the powers of Congress under the Full Faith and Credit Clause, including an essay published by Professor Laurence Tribe in the *New York Times* on May 26, 1996. These arguments are, I believe, baseless.

The Full Faith and Credit Clause was intended by its framers to solidify the Union by requiring each state to respect the laws and legal judgments of sister States. But the Clause has never been understood to impose an absolute obligation; nor could it, given the nature of the subject matter. When two states have inconsistent laws on the same subject, it would literally be impossible for the laws of each to be given effect throughout the country. This would defy the logical principle of noncontradiction. Rather, the Clause was written against the backdrop of choice-of-law principles, including those related to the enforcement of judgments. The effect of the Clause was to subject these principles to federal constitutional review, until and unless Congress has spoken on the

From Michael W. McConnell, written testimony at the Hearing before the Senate Committee on the Judiciary, 104th Cong., 2nd sess., on S. 1740, a bill to define and protect the institution of marriage, July 11, 1996.

subject, and to federal statutory law if Congress so chooses. (Note the use of the permissive verb "may" in the last sentence of the provision.)

The prospect that one state may recognize same-sex unions as "marriages" raises precisely the kind of issue that is properly addressed by Congress under this Clause. Under our Constitution, marriage law is a question left to state law. No state has ever treated same-sex unions as marriages (indeed, no legal jurisdiction in the world has done so). Yet if the State of Hawaii performs marriages of persons of the same sex, these marriages might well be deemed public "Records," and declaratory judgments or other legal proceedings in Hawaii recognizing the validity of any such marriages would almost surely be "Judicial Proceedings," within the meaning of the Full Faith and Credit Clause. It is therefore not unlikely that other states would be compelled to recognize these unions as marriages within their own boundaries. Couples could journey to Hawaii, engage in a marriage ceremony under Hawaii law, and on return to their home states be entitled to legal treatment as a married couple, notwithstanding limitations of marriage in their own home state to persons of the opposite sex. Indeed, one of the briefs in the Hawaii case urges recognition of same-sex marriage precisely because of the bounteous tourist trade this would create.

The prospect that one state may recognize same-sex unions as "marriages" raises precisely the kind of issue that is properly addressed by Congress.

I stress that while this scenario is not unlikely, it also is not certain. It is possible that states with laws against same-sex unions will be able to resist recognition of these marriages under the so-called "public policy" exception. (The answer to this probably hinges on whether marriages are embodied in a legal judgment, or not.) It is also possible that Hawaii will place reasonable domiciliary restrictions on the availability of same-sex marriage. The difficulty, however, is that these issues would not be resolved for many years, and if they are resolved adversely to the interests of the other states, it would likely be too late for Congress to act. The purpose of the proposed act, therefore, is to ensure that each state continues to be able to decide for itself whether to recognize same-sex marriage—to ensure that one state is not able to decide this question, as a practical matter, for the entire nation.

For those who believe in a prudent approach to social change, based on experience rather than abstract theorizing, the proposed statute has the advantage of allowing this rather dramatic departure from past practice to be tested before it is imposed everywhere. While powerful arguments have been made in support of same-sex marriage, the arguments on the other side are not inconsequential. Same-sex marriage has never been tried, and the effects on family, on children, on adoption, on divorce, on adultery rates, and on social mores in general are very difficult to predict. Whatever one's view on the merits of the social question, the advantages of using the "laboratories of democracy" provided by our decentralized, 50-state system, to test the results, before moving to a new national definition of marriage, should be apparent. Yet, if Congress does not act, there is a serious prospect that the Hawaiian definition of marriage will prevail throughout the nation, by virtue of application of the Full Faith and Credit Clause.

Congress has the authority

There is little doubt that Congress has authority to intervene. The Full Faith and Credit Clause explicitly empowers Congress to "prescribe . . . the Effect" that the "public Acts, Records, and Judicial Proceedings" of one state shall have in other states. Congress has rarely exercised this authority, and accordingly there is little precedent (either in the form of legislative interpretations or of judicial decisions) to illuminate it. But there is no reason to doubt that the Clause means precisely what it says: that Congress has plenary power to prescribe what effect the laws of one state will have on another.

The only express limitation on the power of Congress under the Effects Clause is that it must act by "general law." This means that it may not legislate with reference to particular cases. It could not, for example, pass a law specifying that Mr. John Doe's divorce must (or must not) be recognized throughout the Union. Congress should not judge individual cases. The "general law" limitation may also mean that the law must apply to all states. (The term "general" was typically used at the time in contradistinction to "local.") But the proposed Defense of Marriage Act is "general" in every sense of the word. It gives all states the power to enforce their own laws with respect to same-sex marriage.

I have heard it suggested that Congress' power is limited to effectuating or enforcing the acts, records, and judicial proceedings of the states, and that the Defense of Marriage Act does not fall within this category because it denies any effect to certain such acts. This interpretation has no support in the language, purpose, or history of the Clause. To "prescribe the effect" of something is to determine what effect it will have. In the absence of powerful evidence to the contrary, the natural meaning of these words is that Congress can prescribe that a particular class of acts will have no effect at all, or that their effect will be confined to their state of origin.

Congress has plenary power to prescribe what effect the laws of one state will have on another.

In this respect, it is useful to contrast the language of Section Five of the Fourteenth Amendment, which empowers Congress to "enforce, by appropriate legislation, the provisions of this article," or with Article I, §8 cl. 18, which empowers Congress to "make all Laws which shall be necessary and proper for carrying into Execution the foregoing Powers." These provisions are, indeed, limited to statutes that would effectuate their respective purposes. But the Full Faith and Credit Clause is not worded that way. It does not give Congress power to make laws necessary and proper for the "enforcement" of state laws in other states, or for carrying those laws into "execution." Instead, Congress is given full power to "prescribe" their "effect."

There is good reason for this difference. The Full Faith and Credit Clause deals with the problem of inconsistencies in state laws. As noted above, not all state laws can be enforced everywhere, if the laws are in conflict. If Hawaii's law recognizing same-sex marriage is enforced in other states, the laws of those states will be stripped of their efficacy. The field called "choice of law" was developed to deal with these conflicts, and the Full Faith and Credit Clause empowers Congress as the ultimate umpire. But in exercising this power, it necessarily will be the case that Congress gives effect to some state laws and denies effect to others. Thus, an interpretation of the Clause that insists that Congress only has power to "give effect" to state laws and not to "deny effect" is logically impossible. The Defense of Marriage Act may "deny effect" to Hawaiian law under certain circumstances; but by the same token it "gives effect" to the law of the state in which the controversy takes place. The opposite result would "give effect" to Hawaiian law only by "denying effect" to the law of the place in which the conflict takes place.

Until this politically contentious context arose, no scholar studying the meaning of the Full Faith and Credit Clause had ever suggested that Congress' power to prescribe the effect of state laws was impliedly limited in this way. Edward S. Corwin, for example, wrote:

> Congress has the power under the clause to decree the effect that the statutes of one State shall have in other States. This being so, it does not seem extravagant to argue that Congress may under the clause describe a certain type of divorce and say that it shall be granted recognition throughout the Union, and that no other kind shall. Or, to speak in more general terms, Congress has under the clause power to enact standards whereby uniformity of State legislation may be secured as to almost any matter in connection with which interstate recognition of private rights would be useful and valuable.—Edward S. Corwin, *The Constitution and What It Means Today*, 255 (14th ed.).

If Congress can "describe a certain type of divorce and say that it shall be granted recognition throughout the Union" it presumably may describe a certain type of marriage and say the same. See also Walter Wheeler Cook, "The Powers of Congress Under the Full Faith and Credit Clause," 28 *Yale L.J.* 421(1919) (surveying history of the Full Faith and Credit Clause and concluding that it gives Congress full power to determine "the legal effects or consequences in other states of the 'public acts, records and judicial proceedings' of a state," including legislation as well as adjudications); Douglas Laycock, "Equal Citizens of Equal and Territorial States: The Constitutional Foundations of Choice of Law," 92 *Colum. L. Rev.* 249, 331 (1992) ("It is common ground that Congress can designate the authoritative state law under the Effects Clause, specifying which state's law gets any effect in that class of cases"). The proposed Act simply specifies that each state may give effect to its own law in this class of cases.

The argument that the proposed statute would violate the Equal Protection Clause requires little comment. As held in the case of *Romer v. Evans,* 116 S. Ct. 1620, 1627 (1996) laws that disadvantage individuals on the basis of sexual orientation will be upheld so long as they bear "a rational relation to some legitimate end." The provision struck down in *Romer,* the Court held, was not "directed to any identifiable legitimate purpose or discrete objective." *Id.* at 1629. By contrast, it is surely a legitimate legislative purpose to ensure that each state is able to make and enforce its own criteria for recognition of marriage.

Moving beyond the constitutional question, however, I question whether Congress really intends some of the results that could obtain under the proposed Act. For example, if a same-sex couple resident in Hawaii were involved in an automobile accident in Michigan, does it make any sense to treat them as "unmarried" for purposes of tort and insurance law? One way to handle this problem would be to declare that the legal right of two persons to be married to one another is determined by the state of common domicile from time to time, or if there is no common domicile, the state where the relationship is centered. This would leave in place ordinary choice of law rules for cases in which domiciliaries of one state were temporarily present in another state. That would be in keeping with longstanding principles regarding the legal status of "sojourners"—principles that have been honored in the past even in the face of such divisive subjects as slavery.

Please be aware that I write as an individual, and not representing the views of the University of Chicago or of any other group or institution.

Very truly yours,

(Signed) Michael W. McConnell

11

Evidence Supporting Same-Sex Marriages in History Is Inaccurate

Brent D. Shaw

Brent D. Shaw teaches history at the University of Lethbridge in Leth-bridge, Alberta, and is a former member at the Institute for Advanced Study in Princeton, New Jersey, a research and education facility.

John Boswell's claim that the Christian church officially recognized same-sex marriages during the Middle Ages is inaccurate. The ceremonies referred to by Boswell did sanction "same-sex unions," but accurate translations of the original Greek texts show that the rituals served to join unrelated men as "brothers," not as married couples or homosexual lovers.

We find ourselves, all of us, in a historical crisis of gender. It has produced highly charged arguments over "Amendment 2" to the constitution of Colorado, and over the various legal actions that have stemmed from that controversial initiative. [Amendment 2 sought to prohibit state and local governments from banning discrimination on the basis of sexual orientation. The U.S. Supreme Court struck down the amendment in May 1996.] In Ontario, one of the larger provinces in my own country, it has produced acerbic debate and the defeat of a legislative bill that would have recognized same-sex unions as "marital" in nature, and would have granted them comparable rights and duties. No small part of the disputation is about definitions—What is a family? What is a marriage?—and about the social and political consequences of these definitions.

The relationship of historians and their work to this crisis is fraught and dangerous. The stakes are high. And so the appearance of a large book by a well-known historian from Yale University on what are, he says, historical precedents for homosexual marriages in Christian society and their official recognition by the Christian church, is bound to find a large readership and to stoke a vigorous debate. The publisher's announcement

From Brent D. Shaw, "A Groom of One's Own?" *New Republic,* July 18 & 25, 1994. Reprinted by permission of the *New Republic,* ©1994, The New Republic, Inc.

excitedly warns that the work is "bound to be as controversial as the publication of the Dead Sea Scrolls." For John Boswell claims to have discovered a series of medieval manuscripts that record Christian church ceremonials for creating and blessing "same-sex unions"—for what were, in
effect, marriages between men.

Apart from a foray into the problem of abandoned infants in ancient
and early-modern European society, Boswell is best known for his investigation of the problematic relations between male homosexuals and the
Christian church. His *Christianity, Social Tolerance and Homosexuality: Gay
People in Western Europe from the Beginning of the Christian Era to the Fourteenth Century*, which appeared in 1980, was a learned and groundbreaking investigation of a subject that the author rightly categorized as
"taboo." More than twelve years in the researching and writing, his new
book on same-sex unions is similarly intended to reshape our interpretations of the past and our practices in the present.

Boswell attempts to demonstrate that "gay marriage ceremonies"
were an accepted part of the early Christian church, and that the rituals
that formalized such marriages were only later deliberately and consciously effaced by the church. He laudably provides the reader with tran-
scriptions of the documents in the original Greek, along with his own English translations of them. No less laudably, he guides the reader through
interpretations of his material that differ from his own.

A same-sex marriage ceremony

Since the material that Boswell has uncovered is unfamiliar and impres-
sive and controversial, it is perhaps best to give the reader some sense of
it—his own English version of the text of one of these ceremonies. What
follows is from an eleventh-century Greek manuscript labeled Grottaferrata Γ.B. II, and I have inserted some of the significant original Greek
words in transcription.

Office for Same-Sex Union
[*Akolouthia eis adelphopoiesin*]

i.

*The priest shall place the holy Gospel on the Gospel stand and
they that are to be joined together place their right hands on it,
holding lighted candles in their left hands. Then shall the priest
cense them and say the following:*

ii.

In peace we beseech Thee, O Lord.
  For heavenly peace, we beseech Thee, O Lord.
  For the peace of the entire world, we beseech Thee, O
Lord.
  For this holy place, we beseech Thee, O Lord.
  That these thy servants, N. and N., be sanctified with
thy spiritual benediction, we beseech Thee, O Lord.
  That their love [*agape*] abide without offense or scandal

all the days of their lives, we beseech Thee, O Lord.

That they be granted all things needed for salvation and godly enjoyment of life everlasting, we beseech Thee, O Lord.

That the Lord God grant unto them unashamed faithfulness [*pistis*] and sincere love [*agape anhypokritos*], we beseech Thee, O Lord. . . .

Have mercy on us, O God.

"Lord, have mercy" shall be said three times.

iii.

The priest shall say:

Forasmuch as Thou, O Lord and Ruler, art merciful and loving, who didst establish humankind after thine image and likeness, who didst deem it meet that thy holy apostles Philip and Bartholomew be united, bound one unto the other not by nature but by faith and the spirit. As Thou didst find thy holy martyrs Serge and Bacchus worthy to be united together [*adelphoi genesthai*], bless also these thy servants, N. and N., joined together not by the bond of nature but by faith and in the mode of the spirit [*ou desmoumenous desmi physeis alla pisteis kai pneumatikos tropi*], granting unto them peace [*eirene*] and love [*agape*] and oneness of mind. Cleanse from their hearts every stain and impurity and vouchsafe unto them to love one other [*to agapan allelous*] without hatred and without scandal all the days of their lives, with the aid of the Mother of God and all thy saints, forasmuch as all glory is thine.

iv.

Another Prayer for Same-Sex Union

O Lord Our God, who didst grant unto us all those things necessary for salvation and didst bid us to love one another and to forgive each other our failings, bless and consecrate, kind Lord and lover of good, these thy servants who love each other with a love of the spirit [*tous pneumatike agape heautous agapesantas*] and have come into this thy holy church to be blessed and consecrated. Grant unto them unashamed fidelity [*pistis*] and sincere love [*agape anhypokritos*], and as Thou didst vouchsafe unto thy holy disciples and apostles thy peace and love, bestow them also on these, O Christ our God, affording to them all those things needed for salvation and life eternal. For Thou art the light and the truth and thine is the glory.

v.

Then shall they kiss the holy Gospel and the priest and one another, and conclude.

It is this ceremonial, and blessings like these, that Boswell claims to be part of a lost, or deliberately suppressed, tradition of church-legitimized same-sex marriages between men.

Boswell's interpretation

Boswell's argument stands or falls on his interpretation of a series of documents relating to a singular ritual practiced in the Christian church during antiquity and the high middle ages, principally in the lands of the eastern Mediterranean. The bonds between men that are confirmed in these church rituals are cautiously (and a little coyly) labeled by him as "same-sex unions." For his arguments to have the force that he wishes them to have, however, the words "same-sex" and "union" must be construed to mean "male homosexual" and "marriage." If they signify other sorts of associations that happened to be same-sex in gender, or unions that were meant for purposes other than marriage or a permanent affective union, then his claims fail.

For this reason, the narrative chapters of his book are ancillary, in that they digress on other aspects of the general problems of marriage and family formation in a way that is designed to support Boswell's claims about the supposed same-sex marriage rituals. His larger investigation of the nature of "heterosexual" marriage and love, and their attendant vocabulary in the Greco-Roman world, is undertaken to demonstrate that his interpretation of the "same-sex union" rituals is the most probable one.

Given the centrality of Boswell's "new" evidence, therefore, it is best to begin by describing his documents and their import. These documents are liturgies for an ecclesiastical ritual called *adelphopoiesis* or, in simple English, the "creation of a brother." Whatever these texts are, they are not texts for marriage ceremonies. Boswell's translation of their titles (*akolouthia eis adelphopoiesin* and parallels) as "The Order of Celebrating the Union of Two Men" or "Office for Same-Sex Union" is inaccurate. In the original, the titles say no such thing. And this sort of tendentious translation of the documents is found, alas, throughout the book. Thus the Greek words that Boswell translates as "be united together" in the third section of the document quoted above are, in fact, rather ordinary words that mean "become brothers" (*adelphoi genesthai*); and when they are translated in this more straightforward manner, they impart a quite different sense to the reader.

> *There is no indication in the [ecclesiastical] texts themselves that these are marriages in any sense that the word would mean to readers now.*

Whatever effect these liturgical ceremonials were intended to achieve, it is clear that they used ecclesiastical formalities to make two men "brothers," and employed various rituals and symbolic claims to confirm this relationship within the confines of the church. All of Boswell's documents relate to practices rooted in the societies of Greece, the Balkans and the eastern Mediterranean between the twelfth and six-teenth centuries—though, as he rightly argues, they surely reflect practices that were current from periods dating back to the end of the Roman empire, and probably earlier. The original documents that he cites are therefore in Greek, the ecclesiastical lingua franca of the eastern Mediterranean. The only Western versions of them are translations made into Latin from the original Greek prayer and liturgical books—wherein, notably, it seems that the Latin translators did not understand the purpose of the originals very well.

The ecclesiastical rituals that bless *adelphopoiesis*, or the making of a brother, include prayers and invocations of Christian virtues, particularly *agape*, or the Christian concept of love. They note that conditions of peace, not conditions of hate or vituperation, should exist between the two parties. Appeal is also made to pairs of men in the Christian tradition who were thought to exemplify these virtues: Philip and Bartholomew, among the disciples of Christ, and Serge and Bacchus, among the martyrs of the early church. Other elements of the ceremonial include, most significantly, the shaking or "juncture" of right hands; the exchanging of tokens; the mutual bestowing of a ritualistic kiss; and the holding of a celebratory feast or banquet to mark the occasion.

The men often entered into these ["brother"] relationships not out of love, but out of fear and suspicion.

Such agreements and rituals are "same-sex" in the sense that it is two men who are involved; and they are "unions" in the sense that the two men involved are co-joined as "brothers." But that is it. There is no indication in the texts themselves that these are marriages in any sense that the word would mean to readers now, nor in any sense that the word would have meant to persons then: the formation of a common household, the sharing of everything in a permanent co-residential unit, the formation of a family unit wherein the two partners were committed, ideally, to each other, with the intent to raise children, and so on.

Although it is difficult to state precisely what these ritualized relationships were, most historians who have studied them are fairly certain that they deal with a species of "ritualized kinship" that is covered by the term "brotherhood." (This type of "brotherhood" is similar to the ritualized agreements struck between members of the Mafia or other "men of honor" in our own society.) That explains why the texts on *adelphopoiesis* in the prayerbooks are embedded within sections dealing with other kinship-forming rituals, such as marriage and adoption. Giovanni Tomassia in the 1880s and Paul Koschaker in the 1930s, whose works Boswell knows and cites, had already reached this conclusion.

This likely interpretation is made more likely by an extensive modern study of which Boswell appears to be unaware. In 1987 Gabriel Herman, a professor of history at the Hebrew University in Jerusalem, published *Ritualized Friendship and the Greek City*. In that book, and in several papers and articles on the subject published in leading journals of history and literature, Herman has analyzed the phenomenon of fictive "brotherhood" and "friendship" in the context of the world of the Greek city-state, and also in the cultures of the ancient Near East and in the regions that would later become parts of Slavonic Europe. In Herman's studies one finds all the phenomena regarded as indicative of "same-sex marriage" by Boswell: the ritual of the handshake, the exchange of tokens and right hands (*dexiai*), the declarations of love and friendship and of "no hostility or animosity" between the two parties, the exchange of a ritualistic kiss and the celebration of a common feast or banquet at the time of the formation of the compact.

Such ceremonials created ritualized friends who often spoke of each other as "brothers" and forged a close bond of brotherhood between themselves. They were "made brothers" rather than "brothers by nature." Hence the terminology, in Boswell's documents, of *adelphopoiesis*, or the ritual connected with "the making of a brother," and the phrases in his liturgical documents that specify that the two men "are not joined by the bond of nature, but rather by means of faith/trust and spirit," or similar words. This is why the documents contain references to the right of "protective asylum" (*asylon anepereastos*) and "safe conduct" (*asphaleia*) as divine attributes.

The kinds of words used to express the new relationship of "brothers" (words that are also found in Boswell's ecclesiastical rituals) were employed precisely because the men often entered into these relationships not out of love, but out of fear and suspicion. Hence the effusive emphasis on safety and trust. These relationships form as close a parallel in social institutions and practices as one could wish to have as background to the church ceremonials described in the texts cited by Boswell. Although such rituals did create fictive kinship links between the parties to them, these links were never mistaken or confused with the union of marriage. They were not undertaken primarily for erotic or affective reasons, for household formation, nor, even theoretically, for the procreation of children and the continuation of household lines.

There is only one segment of one document in Boswell's book that contains part of a liturgical service designed for a marriage ceremony: the fifth and sixth sections of the Grottaferrata manuscript of the eleventh century. Its words, which do refer to a wedding (*gamos*) and to the ceremonial use of crowns (*stephanoi*) in the ritual "crowning" of the bride and groom, give Boswell grounds to expatiate on the significance of these terms and the ceremonials involved. But there is no mention here of a same-sex union. From even a cursory reading of all of the documents, it is apparent that the original text of the "making of a brother" ceremony terminates at the end of section four of the manuscript in question. What Boswell prints as section five and section six of this document, as if they were a seamless continuation of the ritual of *adelphopoiesis*, belong in fact to an entirely different and separate document, which was indeed connected with a ceremony of marriage. The questionable joining of the two documents as if they were one enables Boswell to appeal throughout his main text to the totality of the documents as if they are all variant types of a marriage ceremonial, which they are not.

Erroneous claims

The rest of Boswell's book does nothing other than provide an interpretive basis for the erroneous claims made about these documents, and there is little in it that is new or significant. His first chapter on "the vocabulary of love and marriage" rightly emphasizes the ambiguity of the terms used to describe love and marriage—he discusses, for example, the strong contextualization of what "to love" or "to kiss" might mean. But tendentious arguments constantly slip into the presentation. Two examples will have to suffice.

To justify the reading of "love" in his sources as having erotic content, Boswell has to demonstrate that the noun *agape*, "love," and the verb *agapan*, "to love," could be used to describe any sort of love relationship, including a wholly erotic one. This is clearly not the case. Any thorough study of the term *agape* will justify the traditional view that this was an unusual Christian coinage when applied to love. It signaled, as a novel virtue, an ability to accept and to embrace one's entire condition as a part of a millennially transformed world. As Boswell himself notes, the vocabulary of pre-Christian physical and sexual love—for example, the verb *eran*, meaning to love erotically—is almost wholly absent from the New Testament. Although the Christian term *agape* did occasionally enter the discourse of other late Greek writers as an alternative manner of expressing physical or erotic love, such usages are extremely rare. But that is hardly the point. What remains indisputable is the significance of the word in ecclesiastical, theological and liturgical writings—in the specific genres of Boswell's "same-sex union" documents.

> *Love and affection [and] . . . the procreation of children . . . were central to the Roman concept and the Roman practice of marriage.*

Another misleading lexical interpretation is Boswell's treatment of the word *adelphos* or "brother." He believes that the word "brother" designates a homosexual lover. "The term 'brother,'" he writes, "was widely understood in the Roman world to denote a permanent partner in a homosexual relationship." This is a possible meaning in some genres (in, say, Greco-Roman romantic novels); but context must be given priority in interpretation, since it is context that determines the meaning that was normally to be understood. One cannot abuse a mere possibility as sufficient grounds for asserting that a word, in this instance the word "brother," must have had precisely this significance in a series of Christian liturgical texts.

Boswell's tendency to misconstrue evidence extends beyond simple matters of definition, however, to the very social institutions that are central to his analysis. So, in his treatment of "heterosexual matrimony" in the Greco-Roman world, he is careless not only with proofs and concepts, but also with modern vocabulary. To label matrimony in Roman society as "heterosexual," as Boswell consistently labels it, is misleading, since it suggests that there was some form of "homosexual" matrimony recognized by the same social order. The plain fact is that there never was such a formally acknowledged alternative. Boswell describes marriages in Roman society as things that were "primarily a property arrangement" or "business deals"; he claims that "divorce was very common"; and, perhaps most astoundingly, he asserts that "children were not integral to the ideal of marriage." A brief consideration of some of the best documented upper-class families of the period, such as the family of Cicero, will readily demonstrate that even on this highly property-conscious level of society, marriage and marital relationships can hardly be reduced to the crude scheme presented by Boswell.

As for the purpose of producing children, what else can one add when the *tabulae nuptiales*, or marital agreements, which were part of the contractual arrangements between the married couple, specifically stated, in conformity with the norms espoused by "pagan" philosophers and Christian bishops and theologians, that marriage was primarily intended for the procreation of children, or *liberorum procreandorum causa*? In all these matters, Boswell creates a portrait of "heterosexual" marriages that is a caricature, and not at all a fair reflection of the day-to-day realities of such unions. Although he frequently cites Susan Treggiari's *Roman Marriage*, the most recent comprehensive analysis of matrimony in the Roman world, Boswell ignores Treggiari's basic findings: that love and affection, a type of (admittedly asymmetrical) sexual fidelity between the partners, the procreation of children, the sharing of resources, the hope of a lifelong union only to be ended by death and other such ideals were central to the Roman concept and the Roman practice of marriage.

It must be admitted that the problems and readings of family history faced by Boswell are of a very high order of difficulty. The best historians who have tried to cope with definitions of marriage and the family in the past have often found themselves in an obstinate morass, for past practices were no less diverse and nebulous than those of the present, and the gap between ideological presentations of family life and the realities of family life was no less difficult to gauge. One can no more speak of *the* model Roman family than one can speak of the model American family today. The potential variation was great. Then, as now, the model of what a family was relied upon tacit negative definitions or assumptions about what it was not.

Still, the definitions that we do have, the pre-Christian Roman ones, legal and literary, and the later Christian theological and canonical ones, are unanimous in regarding marriage or *matrimonium* invariably as a union of opposite sexes: male and female. The core Roman legal definition of marriage is explicit on the matter. It quite consciously and deliberately does not refer to distinctions of social status (husband and wife as *maritus* and *uxor*), or even to those of gender (man and woman as *vir* and *femina*), but instead it rather carefully refers to sexual differences, and defines marriage as the joining of male and female, *coniunctio maris et feminae*. (I refer to *Digest*, 23.2.11, and also 1.1.3, where marriage is explicitly associated with the procreation of children.)

This sexual definition was explicit and constant, while the romantic, loving or affective elements were variable. Hence different expectations of such a union are expressed; but no possibility is ever considered other than one constituted of these basic elements. Similarly, what a family was varied in terms of space, time, life cycle, region, culture and social class. It began with postulates of marriage and family formation by means of children, but it then diverged from these central assumptions and legal definitions. A single man, if he was a legally autonomous person, together with his household of personal slaves, would constitute a *familia*. There were numerous deviations, then, from the core definition, numerous possibilities; but there were always limits, negative frontiers were always encountered and beyond them there never existed any conception that the union of two males could possibly constitute a family—even in cases of the *frereche*, the consortium or sharing of property between two unmarried brothers.

As in most historical societies, formal definitions, elastic practices and assumed boundaries regarding family and marriage existed simultaneously in Rome. Some of them stood in manifest contradiction. One of the dominant models of the Roman *familia* in the legal codes was that of a multigenerational male descent lineage under the domination of a very powerful and senior household head, the "father of the family" or *paterfamilias*. But the tendency of most Roman families that were not in the propertied elite, and that formed the majority of the population in the cities and towns of the empire, was to the continual re-forming of small "nuclear" or elementary families. The power elite, needless to say, lived in a rather different sexual and familial world, and it is the world that overwhelmingly dominates our surviving literary records. It would be a mistake to take the legally prescriptive texts of the wealthy and the powerful as offering realistic definitions of family and marriage for most persons in this society. While recognizing some of the complexity of Roman marriage and family patterns, Boswell leaves the matter there. He does not advance to an explicit recognition of the fact that, all the haziness notwithstanding, there were well-known and firmly set boundaries to the conception and the conduct of marriage in the Roman world.

Out of context

To sustain his argument, Boswell must constantly tear words, sentences and larger statements out of the social and literary contexts in which they were embedded. Of this, I will give only a single example, but it is a particularly characteristic one. The essay titled *Toxaris*, which was composed by the second-century Greek writer Lucian, is invoked several times by Boswell to demonstrate the intense homoerotic content of unions formed between two men, and to sustain one of his arguments that such "friendships" were in fact male marriages. The problem is that a few lines or paragraphs wrenched from the context of the whole work impart a distorted picture to the reader of what is actually happening.

Lucian's essay is a fictitious dialogue between a Greek called Mnesippos and a Scythian named Toxaris on the subject of "friendship" (*philia*) between men. It is not just any sort of friendship, however, but precisely the sort of "ritualized" or fictive friendship between two powerful and potentially hostile men that has been cogently analyzed by Herman. Whatever homoerotic feelings and sentiments might have been part of the affective content of such a relationship, and there is no denying that in some cases homosexual men may have found emotional satisfaction in such socially sanctioned "friendship," this does not add up to an understanding of the social institution itself, and it certainly does not make it a "same-sex union" in the sense of being a marriage. It is this kind of decontextualization that permits Boswell to string together isolated pieces of evidence that lead him in the wrong direction.

The text of Lucian's *Toxaris* is important, since Boswell uses it as a critical proof for one of "three types of formal unions," of which "more detail is known." This union, he argues at length, was a type of same-sex union of two men, explicitly stating that it is a strict analogue to "heterosexual" marriage. The positive evidence that Boswell adduces in support of same-sex marriage practices is worth examining in detail. As the Scythian Toxaris makes clear in his summation of Mnesippos's examples of "friendship" between men in Greek societies of the time, such friendships permit these men to achieve heroic deeds. But note what such accomplishments are: marrying an ugly wife without a dowry, giving money to the amount of two talents to the daughter of a friend on her marriage, and the sharing of a period of temporary imprisonment.

When the Scythian Toxaris gives examples of male *philia* in his own society, he begins by noting that the Greeks "have no great occasions at all" on which to display their *philia* because they live in conditions of "profound peace," or *eirene batheia*. The Scythians, by contrast, are constantly involved in war and fighting. The words of Toxaris that follow are worth quoting not only because Boswell repeatedly avers to them, but also because they provide us with one of the closest analogues to the relationship referred to in his ecclesiastical documents:

> First of all, I wish to tell you how we make our friends. Not through being drinking buddies, like you people do, not because a man has been in army cadet training with us [*synephebos*] and not because he's our neighbor. No. When we see a brave man capable of achieving great things, it's then that we all become eager to get close to him. And just as you behave when you are trying to get married, we think it right to behave in this same way in forming friends— wooing them at great length and with much effort, and doing everything to ensure that we do not lose their friendship and are rejected. Then when the decision has been made to accept someone as a friend [*philos*], an agreement is made and a great oath is sworn that we will live together and, if necessary, even die for each other. We actually do this. For when we have cut our fingers, let the blood drip into a cup, dipped our sword points into it and then, together, both at the same time have raised it to our lips and have drunk, there is nothing that happens afterwards that can possibly break the link between us. We are allowed to enter into three such alliances at most, since we think that a man who has [too] many friends [*polyphilos*] is like immoral and adulterous women, and we consider that the strength of his friendship is no longer the same when it has been split between [too] many loyalties [*pollai eunoiai*].

This is a distorting "colonialist" fiction, a Greek writer imagining what the barbarians do, and therefore a literary interpretation of the lived realities of Scythian life. Still, there is enough in the account that is reliable to make a basic assumption in it clear: that the fictional Scythian speaker is not referring to anything like same-sex male marriages, but rather to an intense social bond that was formed between men of power for the purpose of coping with the lack of formal institutions in their society and the violent behavior that pervaded it. He likens the actions undertaken by Scythian men in forming this bond to the sorts of rituals used by the civilized and peaceful Greeks in the pursuit of the women whom they wish to make their wives. But the comparison is clearly and forcefully signaled as a metaphor, as a social simile. Scythian "friendship" is clearly not marriage, since most of the men are described as having wives and children, and Toxaris's third story of such a "friendship" involves three "friends" assisting one of their own to achieve a marriage—to help the man in the successful pursuit of the woman whom he loves and wishes to wed.

Toxaris specifically states that the purposes of forming such male alliances are personal protection and violence: raiding; the conduct of wars and vengeance; the protection of possessions of herds, pasture lands and wagons; the defense of community. He provides illustrations of how such ritual friendship or *philia* allows men to marshal the resources of kin and friends to assemble whole armies, and to use the ascribed power of blood rituals, compacts, promises and exchanges of tokens to control resources vital to their survival. The details of this *philia* given by Toxaris sometimes involve three men simultaneously, though it is clear that such men also have families, wives and children and other species of property that these personal alliances were meant to protect and to subserve. These "friendships" are specifically stated as giving men power to effect aims that they would not be able to achieve on their own. But here is Boswell's recapitulation of these *philia* relationships between Scythian men:

> They [artificial kinship relations] were often, for example, symbolic ratifications of peace, pledges of cooperation between warriors or peoples, or means of forming ties between families or tribes. . . . But there is absolutely no suggestion of any of these functions in Toxaris's description of the Scythian practice . . . there is no indication that any other family or tribal members are involved; and the bond is not presented as political or strategic, or as having any broader social significance than personal emotional attachment. Its significance is manifestly and unmistakably personal and affectional.

Apart from Boswell's hyperbolic denials of direct statements in the *Toxaris*, there is little I can say except that he and I must be reading different texts.

Adoption

Boswell then juxtaposes three texts from Roman legal codes and claims that they demonstrate his "third type of formal same-sex union," which involved the legal practice of "collateral adoption": one man adopted another as his brother and hence as a marital partner. These matters are legal and complex, and it is best to take them in turn. The first text (*Digest*, 38.2.59) says nothing at all about adoption. It merely states the conditions under which a person can nominate someone as an heir to his or her property. The jurist Paul then adds that if someone is not a biological brother but you treat him as one, you may call the person by the name "brother" when you designate him as heir, and the testament will still be valid. That is all. There is nothing said about adopting the person. The second passage (*Digest*, 38.8.3) does indeed mention "adoptive brothers," but from the context it seems clear that the jurist is treating nothing other than the ordinary problem of siblings, one of whom might happen to be adopted, and the consequences that would follow from this fact for inheritance.

[The core Roman legal definition of marriage] rather carefully refers to sexual differences, and defines marriage as the joining of male and female.

So far, therefore, there is no evidence whatever for adult males adopting other adult men as their brothers. The singular reference to such a possibility is contained in a late third-century legal decision issued by the Roman emperors (*Codex Justinianus*, 6.24.7). It is a solitary case referring to an eastern Mediterranean context that was not understood by the emperors themselves. In any event, they denied the legal validity of the attempt at fraternal adoption. That is it. Boswell then claims that scholars have deliberately refused to consider the institution of adult men adopting other men as their "brothers" as a formal type of homosexual union, "because it could not be honestly considered in the moral and intellectual climate of Europe or the United States in the last two centuries." "The only convincing explanation for collateral adoption," he continues, "would seem to be its peculiar personal and emotional value, about which scholars writing in the last century have shown so slight a curiosity as to border on aversion." This verges on paranoia. Except for one brief imperial legal decision, there is no evidence for the supposed institutional practice of adult male adoption as a form of same-sex marriage. The uniqueness and the lack of context of that one legal ruling, and not any malign conspiracy of silence, are more than sufficient to account for the lack of scholarly curiosity.

Boswell's analysis of the Christian church and matrimony is designed to downplay the former's concerns with family formation and marriage, and thus to reduce the latter to a more secular, contractual relationship that would be more easily transferable to "same-sex unions." He ends his discussion with an extensive analysis of the late antique and early medieval hagiographical accounts of the Roman soldier-martyrs Serge and Bacchus. The data adduced are peculiar selections that favor his own interpretation. Thus, in Boswell's words, the public parading of miscreants as a punishment either by itself, or as a prelude to execution, "does recall the penalty for homosexual acts described by Procopius, Malalas and Theophanes." Those authors alluded to the same ritualistic punishment for pederastic relations. But the fact is that this punishment was in no way especially limited to persons committing "homosexual acts." Public exposure, and the humiliation achieved by parading criminals through public streets, was habitually enforced on many types of outcasts in the Roman empire, including Christians. The use of the punishment might hint at an element of homoerotic relations between Serge and Bacchus, but not necessarily, since the entire martyrological account has them executed because they were Christians and for no other reason.

Boswell's analysis of "same-sex unions" is on firmer ground when he creates a typology that extends from males who were sexually exploited by other men because they were dominated or owned by them to free and volitional relationships between male lovers. But the leap to the formation of permanent relations that were in fact marital—"the fourth type of homosexual relationship known in the ancient world consisted of formal unions"—is not underwritten by any solid or persuasive data. Almost all his examples are ones repeated from his first book—for example, the vituperative attacks by the imperial biographer Suetonius and the historian Tacitus on the extravagant behavior of Nero, including his "marriage" to one Sporus. But neither Suetonius nor Tacitus regards this "union" as a genuine marriage, and the entire effect of their explicit condemnation of Nero's behavior is founded on the assumption that their readers share the same view.

Language, context and assumed meaning clearly show that the other Roman authors cited by Boswell, including the satirist Martial, were never remotely referring to a separate and parallel sphere of male "same-sex marriages," but rather to what they perceived as a perversion of the only known, and acceptable, type of marriage. That is what made their satire work. It was designed, after all, as an aggressive attack on the character of the disparaged person. Hence it is astounding to see Boswell reach the conclusion, on the basis of a single passage from Juvenal's *Satires*, that homosexual marriages were "absolutely commonplace." If that were so, Juvenal's lines would lack the wit and the mordant punch that were obviously intended by their author. Such lapses are, alas, too frequent in Boswell's attempt to provide a literary and historical basis for his argument. Boswell translates a passage from the Greek historian Xenophon as "the man and the boy live together like married people," only to admit in a footnote that "like married people is not literally expressed." In fact, the words are not in the original at all; they are gratuitously provided by Boswell.

A misleading reading

The practices and the rituals performed by the men in Boswell's documents, and also the emotional and erotic connections that are so richly described by him, may seem unusual or frightening to us, given our codes of civility, morality and masculinity. There is a nice irony here: the ancient and medieval world about which Boswell writes was not riven by the same anxieties and repressions that mark our own. In that world, public and affective bonds between men were typical, even banal. But this is not the same thing as the legitimization, or the sacralization, of homosexuality. The "new" documents that Boswell has unearthed are nothing more than a few additional texts that shed more light on a primitive and basic power linkage between men in the ancient Mediterranean, and the rituals attendant on its formation.

By the time Boswell's ecclesiastical documents celebrated or blessed this type of personal arrangement, it had been brought at least partially under the aegis of the Christian church. As the structures of the law and the civil institutions of the state became more dominant, particularly in Western Europe, the church wished to divest itself of a ceremonial that was intended to substantiate a type of personal power that, in synchrony with the state, it now excoriated. Ritualized friendship naturally survived much longer in parts of the eastern Mediterranean, and especially in the mountainous regions of the Balkans, where more primitive forms of personal power have tended to subsist. There might well have been homo-erotic elements to some of these "brotherhood" relationships, and a rather alien Greek ritual may have been misunderstood by some of its Latin translators; both of those possibilities deserve more attention than they have received by historians. But same-sex marriages forged with the approval of the Christian church, and with its rituals? No. Such a reading is very misleading.

The data of the past may not be all that happy for the liberationist movements of our time. Why else would those movements come into being? But what the sources record is, for better or for worse, what the sources record. A good part of what they record, certainly, is made up of systematic and successful repressions; but tinkering with the moral balance of the past is a disservice to the study of history and to the reform of society. The past is dead. We cannot change it. What we can change is the future; but the way to a better future requires an unsentimental and accurate understanding of what happened in the past, and why. A more civil and humane modernity will not be achieved by tendentious mis-readings of antiquity.

12

The Purpose of Marriage Is Procreation

Commonweal

Commonweal *is a biweekly Catholic magazine.*

Historically, the purpose of marriage was the conceiving and raising of children. Contemporary views of marriage, however, have emphasized personal fulfillment over the care of children. Society's acceptance of abortion, premarital sex, and birth control have further eroded the connection between marriage and procreation. Legalizing same-sex marriage would further destabilize and trivialize the institution of marriage.

There is every likelihood that Hawaii's Supreme Court will soon overturn that state's prohibition on same-sex marriage. [A Hawaiian trial court legalized same-sex marriage in December 1996.] The court's reasoning will be simple enough: Hawaii's constitution forbids discrimination on the basis of sex, and for the state to deny the benefits of marriage to same-sex couples without demonstrating a "compelling state interest" does precisely that. Should Hawaii license same-sex marriage, other states may be bound to recognize those marriages under the Full Faith and Credit clause of the Constitution. The U. S. Supreme Court, it seems certain, will eventually be asked to rule on the constitutionality of the heterosexual exclusivity of marriage.

For the state to license same-sex unions will entail a fundamental reappraisal of the nature of marriage and the balance struck between rights of individual self-determination and the integrity of basic social institutions such as the family. American society has much to gain from a fair-minded debate about such questions, and much to lose if we retreat further from reasoning together about the nature and aims of our common life.

The nature of marriage

Whether there are compelling enough reasons to preserve the heterosexual exclusivity of marriage is a question that arises in the wake of pro-

From "Marriage's True Ends," Editorial, *Commonweal*, May 17, 1996. Reprinted with permission.

found changes in how we think about sexual morality, procreation, and marriage. Historically, marriage forged a powerful connection between sexual love, procreation, and the care of children. However, contemporary understandings of marriage increasingly stress the primacy of individual self-fulfillment, not intergenerational attachments. Moreover, contraception and abortion have essentially severed any unwilled connection between sex and procreation. That connection has been further attenuated by technological advances allowing us to separate biological, gestational, and relational parenting at will. In this context, marriage's meaning seems anything but secure.

But is a further erosion of marriage's traditional linkage between sexual love and human procreation desirable? Advocates of same-sex marriage advance two arguments. First, denying same-sex couples the marriage rights enjoyed by heterosexual persons is discriminatory, an imposition of unjustified inequality. Second, same-sex marriage is presented as an embrace of, not an assault on, what is acknowledged to be a uniquely valuable social institution. If society wishes to promote the human goods of marriage—emotional fulfillment, lifelong commitment, the creation of families, and the care of children—marginalizing homosexuals by denying civil standing to their publicly committed relationships makes little sense, advocates argue.

In modern democratic societies wide latitude is given to individuals and groups pursuing often conflicting and incompatible conceptions of the good. Still, a broad tolerance and a high regard for individual autonomy cannot result in the equal embrace of every private interest or social arrangement. Economic freedom, for example, must be balanced against environmental concerns. Parents' rights to instill their own values in their children must accommodate the state's mandate to set educational standards for all children. The exclusive legal status of monogamous marriage, it is useful to remember, was once challenged by Mormon polygamy. But polygamy was judged inimical to the values of individual dignity and social comity that marriage uniquely promotes.

We are all the offspring of a man and a woman, and marriage is the necessary moral and social response to that natural human condition.

Now we must weigh the implicit individual and social benefits of heterosexual marriage against those of same-sex unions. In this light, advocates of same-sex marriage often argue that laws prohibiting it are analogous to miscegenation statutes. But the miscegenation analogy fails. Miscegenation laws were about racial separation, not about the nature of marriage. Legalizing same-sex unions will not remedy a self-evident injustice by broadening access to the traditional goods of marriage. Rather, same-sex marriage, like polygamy, would change the very nature and social architecture of marriage in ways that may empty it of any distinctive meaning.

Recent social history can guide us here. Proponents of no-fault divorce argued that the higher meaning of marriage, and even the health of children, would be better served in making marriage easier to dissolve. Yet the plight of today's divorced women and their children refutes such claims. In fact, the loosening of marital bonds and expectations has contributed to the devaluation and even the abandonment of the marriage ideal by many, while encouraging unrealistic expectations of marriage for many more. How society defines marriage has a profound effect on how individuals think and act. And how individuals fashion their most intimate relationships has an enormous impact on the quality of our common life. The dynamic involved is subtle, but real.

Should marriage be essentially a contractual arrangement between two individuals to be defined as they see fit? Or does marriage recognize and embody larger shared meanings that cannot be lightly divorced from history, society, and nature—shared meanings and social forms that create the conditions in which individuals can achieve their own fulfillment? Popular acceptance of premarital sex and cohabitation gives us some sense of the moral and social trajectory involved. Both developments were welcomed as expressions of greater honesty and even better preparations for marriage. Yet considerable evidence now suggests that these newfound "freedoms" have contributed to the instability and trivialization of marriage itself, and have not borne the promises once made for them of happier lives. Similarly, elevating same-sex unions to the same moral and legal status as marriage will further throw into doubt marriage's fundamental purposes and put at risk a social practice and moral ideal vital to all.

The procreative marriage

The heterosexual exclusivity of marriage can be defended in the same way social policy rightly shows a preference for the formation of intact two-parent families. In both cases, a normative definition of family life is indispensable to any coherent and effective public action. Certainly, mutual love and care are to be encouraged wherever possible. But the justification and rationale for marriage as a social institution cannot rest on the goods of companionship alone. Resisting such a reductionist understanding is not merely in the interests of heterosexuals. There are profound social goods at stake in holding together the biological, relational, and procreative dimensions of human love.

"There are countless ways to 'have' a child," writes theologian Gilbert Meilaender of the social consequences and human meaning of procreation (*Body, Soul, & Bioethics*, University of Notre Dame Press, 1996). "Not all of them amount to doing the same thing. Not all of them will teach us to discern the equal humanity of the child as one who is not our product but, rather, the natural development of shared love, like to us in dignity. . . . To conceive, bear, give birth to, and rear a child ought to be an affirmation and a recognition: affirmation of the good of life that we ourselves were given; recognition that this life bears its own creative power to which we should be faithful."

Is there really any doubt that in tying sexual attraction to love and love to children and the creation of families, marriage fundamentally shapes our ideas of human dignity and the nature of society? Same-sex marriage, whatever its virtues, would narrow that frame and foreshorten our perspective. Marriage, at its best, tutors us as no other experience can in the given nature of human life and the acceptance of responsibilities we have not willed or chosen. Indeed, it should tutor us in respect for the given nature of homosexuality and the dignity of homosexual persons. With this respect comes a recognition of difference—a difference with real consequences.

Still, it is frequently objected that if the state does not deny sterile or older heterosexual couples the right to marry, how can it deny that right to homosexual couples, many of whom are already rearing children?

Exceptions do not invalidate a norm or the necessity of norms. How some individuals make use of marriage, either volitionally or as the result of some incapacity, does not determine the purpose of that institution. In that context, heterosexual sterility does not contradict the meaning of marriage in the way same-sex unions would. If marriage as a social form is first a procreative bond in the sense that Meilaender outlines, then marriage necessarily presupposes sexual differentiation, for human procreation itself presupposes sexual differentiation. We are all the offspring of a man and a woman, and marriage is the necessary moral and social response to that natural human condition. Consequently, sexual differentiation, even in the absence of the capacity to procreate, conforms to marriage's larger design in a way same-sex unions cannot. For this reason sexual differentiation is marriage's defining boundary, for it is the precondition of marriage's true ends.

13

Same-Sex Marriage Is Not True Marriage

The Religion & Society Report

The Religion & Society Report *is a monthly periodical of the Rockford Institute, an educational organization that promotes Judeo-Christian and traditional family values.*

A Hawaiian judge's decision that it is unconstitutional to deny gays and lesbians the right to marry contradicts the laws of God and nature. Throughout recorded history, marriage has been the union of a man and a woman. No society recognizes marriage between two members of the same sex. Despite the judge's order, the union of two men or two women will never make a genuine marriage.

At the end of the nineteenth century, the United States, bent on manifest destiny, seized a small Pacific Ocean island kingdom populated by Polynesians. Until the Japanese attack that brought the United States into World War II, the island territory enjoyed a sort of drowsy tranquility. In the middle of the twentieth century, the islands were given U.S. statehood. Now, at the end of the twentieth century, the little conquered kingdom, now a U.S. state, has suddenly shown the potential to destabilize the entire civilized order of the once dominant mainland.

Overturning human history

An Asian-American federal circuit judge in Hawaii, Kevin S.C. Chang, has ruled that it is unconstitutional for the State of Hawaii to refuse marriage licenses to "gay"[1] and lesbian couples. Calling the ban unconstitutional, the judge ordered the state to stop denying marriage licenses to same-sex couples. One might reasonably object that marriage is a divine ordinance and part of the order of nature and that, in consequence, the state should have nothing to say about it, but for untold generations it has been the custom of organized human societies to protect and stabilize the male-female unions that begin human families.

With a stroke of the pen, Judge Chang overturned six thousand years

From "Ego, Judex," Editorial, *Religion and Society Report*, March 1997. Reprinted with permission.

of recorded human history, the religious teachings of Judaism and Christianity, the philosophical presuppositions of Confucianism, the will of both the state legislature of Hawaii and of the populace as expressed in polls, and the existence of which contravenes both the laws of God and of nature. If a judge, by virtue of the established principles of judicial dictatorship, has the power to turn society on its head, who can reasonably deny him the pleasure of doing it?

It must be an awful, almost irresistible temptation for a judge to be offered the choice of overthrowing the order of millennia or leaving a millennial *status quo* in place. Supreme Court Justice Ruth Bader Ginsburg could not resist the temptation to destroy a century and one-half of tradition at V.M.I. [Virginia Military Institute] and the Citadel in the name of constitutional rights never envisaged by the Founders and certainly not explicitly contained in the text of the Constitution. How can we expect a single district judge, possessing the power to overturn the laws of both God and nature, to resist when an opportunity presents itself?

Judge Chang did this on the basis of a document adopted by the representatives of a small nation just emerging from colonialism, with a population barely one-seventieth that of the United States of today. Should the will of a scant four million newly independent former colonials, expressed in a document of a few pages and interpreted or manipulated at will by judges, prevail over the will of the people as expressed in elections and referenda? We have seen that it does, in *Romer v. Evans* which set aside a referendum in Colorado, in decisions pending in California (on illegal immigration and affirmative action), in Arizona (on English as the official language), and elsewhere, but until now we have not seen a judge tell us that his judgment must prevail over the laws of God and nature.

Marriage is, and always has been, . . . a union between male and female.

Judge Chang did this by interpreting the document in a sense that would have seemed as absurd to its drafters as a ruling declaring that it is a violation of the Constitution for dogs not to be enabled to climb trees. Precedent clearly meant nothing to him. The common law principle of *stare decisis,* of standing by those things that have been decided, evidently carries no weight with a man armed with the power to move the earth—or at least to declare that legally the earth has been moved simply by a few words from his pen.

The state's attorneys, seeking to defend the old order—"Marriage is an honorable estate, established by God, regulated by His commandments . . ."—presented only weak, utilitarian arguments: it is better for children to have two parents of different sexes than two of the same sex. Overlooking the natural tie between generations, which results from the fact that it takes two parents of different sexes to produce a child, so that the only *natural* place for a child is within a family created by the union of a man and a woman, the state's attorneys argued that it is qualitatively better for parents to be of two sexes. This is no doubt true, but it is a weak argument and totally overlooks the fundamental issue: namely, what marriage actually is in the order of God and of nature. Marriage *is*, and always has been, since humans have learned to record their doings, a union between male and female. In the various cultures of the earth there are polygamous marriages, generally with a plurality of wives, occasionally with a plurality of husbands, but there is no such thing as a marriage between two persons of the same sex, between two men or two women.

Not a marriage

Judge Chang may order the State of Hawaii to issue marriage licenses, but no license issued by the state, no matter how numerous or exalted the judges that order it, can make a union between two men or two women a marriage, any more than a court decree or legislative enactment can make a cow into a horse or a bat into a bird. We might well paraphrase Satan's boast in Milton's *Paradise Lost,*

> The Court is its own place, and can make
> a Heav'n of Hell, a Hell of Heaven.

Twenty states and the federal government have already enacted laws defining marriage as what it is, namely, the union between a man and a woman. Now, with Judge Chang's decision, the legal observers on television and in the print media tell us that the issue will go to the courts to be decided for all mankind, or at least for all those over whom the American judiciary holds sway. Although there is no apparent connection, there is a precedent in *Roe v. Wade,* the great abortion decision of the Supreme Court (1973). In *Roe,* the court claimed not to know what every student of biology must know, namely, that life, including human life, begins with the union of a human sperm and egg. Now Judge Chang, perhaps soon to be followed by judges and justices of higher or even the highest rank, has declared that marriage is not what every human being until now has known it to be, the union of male and female.

The media have shown us, as to be expected, touching pictures of loving same-sex couples, weeping tears of joy at their "victory." It would seem that only the cruel and hard-hearted can begrudge them this success. The usual chorus of voices will be raised, telling us that it is far better to help such lovers to live in mutual fidelity and harmony than to doom them to a shadowy life outside the law, and perhaps to leave them prone to infidelity and promiscuity. Indeed, it may in fact be better for society for two homosexual men, for example, to live faithfully with one another than to roam the highways and byways of promiscuous sex. It certainly is far less likely to spread the plague of AIDS. But even so, it is not marriage. As long as the feeble defenders of the divine and natural order limit themselves to arguing that two-sex marriage is somewhat preferable to single-sex unions, it is unlikely that sanity will prevail in the courts.

I, the Judge, have spoken: Let every man a woman be, and every dog a cat.

Note

1. Some readers have questioned our practice of frequently, if not always, placing the word "gay," with reference to male homosexuality, in quotation

marks. There are two reasons for this; first, the older and primary meaning of the word was different, and this older meaning should not simply be abandoned. Second, when reference is being made to statutes and court decisions, as in the article above, it is questionable to use what is essentially a slang expression instead of a legally precise one. The persistent use of the word "gay" instead of the older and more appropriate words "deviant" or "unnatural" indicates a favorable judgment of the practice, for who among us would prefer to be gloomy?

14

Same-Sex Marriage Would Destroy the Institution of Marriage

Hadley Arkes

Hadley Arkes is the Ney Professor of Jurisprudence at Amherst College in Massachusetts and a contributing editor of the National Review. *He was a consultant in the litigation over gay rights in Cincinnati.*

Recent court cases at the state level threaten to open the door to the legalization of same-sex marriage throughout America. However, marriage is defined by nature as the sexual coupling of a man and a woman for the purpose of conceiving children. Legalizing gay marriage would separate marriage from its foundation in nature and would thereby remove the basis for banning other forms of marriage, such as incestuous or polygamous unions.

Editor's note: Hadley Arks testified for the Defense of Marriage Act before the House Judiciary Committee's Subcommittee on the Constitution on May 15, 1996. The act was signed into law by Bill Clinton in September 1996.

A braham Lincoln once remarked, with an unwarranted modesty, that he had been more controlled by events rather than commanding, on his own, the power to control them. That we are meeting in 1996 to discuss the definition of "marriage" in the federal code, or the question of "same-sex marriage," is something that even the most prescient among us could hardly have anticipated three or four years ago. That it should require any further need to explain in the law that a "marriage" means a relation between a man and a woman, is something that could barely have been imagined even then. This is not a subject we have sought out with high spirits, or even a subject that we have been overly willing to speak about, in private settings or public. And yet, it is a subject that has been pressed on us by events. Or to be slightly more exact, it has been pressed on us by the judges and courts and the movement of litigation.

From Hadley Arkes, testimony at the Hearing before the Subcommittee on the Constitution, House Committee on the Judiciary, 104th Cong., 2nd sess., on H.R. 3396, Defense of Marriage Act, May 15, 1996.

Colorado and Cincinnati

I am not referring here to the litigation famously ripening in Hawaii since the early 1990s. The politics of Hawaii have been churning about the question of gay marriage, but it appears that the legislature in Hawaii will produce no decisive judgment, and that this matter will be played out within the cast determined by the courts. That course seems as predictable today as it was when the Court in Hawaii came forth with its decision in *Baehr v. Lewin* [852 P.2d 44 (1993)]: The Equal Rights Amendment to the constitution of the state is likely to be taken finally as a bar to any refusal to tender a license of marriage to a couple of the same sex. It will likely be found, in the end, that the state can supply no compelling interest to offset this presumptive conclusion, which is taken now to spring from the constitution of the state. And of course, even the most emphatic expression of sentiment, conveyed in a statute, would still not override a principle that is thought to be planted in the Constitution. Barring, then, a constitutional amendment, we must reasonably expect that the state of Hawaii will soon deliver, as its gift to the nation, this novelty called "same-sex marriage." Timing is all, and it remains mainly for the judges to determine, with their exquisite political sensitivities, the most apt moment for springing their creation.

Were the notion of marriage so altered as to accommodate [gay activists], the move would set off deeper changes in the definition of marriage.

In the meantime, local newspapers in Washington have borne ads for groups running charters to Hawaii for couples with an interest in marrying under this new regime. The expectation, of course, is that the Full Faith and Credit clause of the Constitution [Article IV, Section 1] may help them bring their marriages back to their States on the mainland.

But all of that has been in the making since 1993, and it is not the momentum of that litigation in Hawaii that accounts for the sense of urgency and brings forth, in 1996, this bill for the Defense of Marriage. The spur to act in this season has been supplied by the rocky litigation over gay rights in Colorado and Cincinnati. Both cases involve constitutional amendments—to the constitution of the state in Colorado, and the city charter in Cincinnati. In both cases, the voters sought to put beyond the reach of legislators the authority to treat gays and lesbians as a victimized class on the same plane as the groups that have suffered discrimination on the basis of race, religion or gender. The vehicle in both instances was a measure that barred legislatures from creating, for gays and lesbians, "any claim of minority or protected status, quota preference or other preferential treatment." So read Amendment II in Colorado, and with slight differences, Issue 3 in Cincinnati. Amendment II was held invalid [in 1996] by the Supreme Court of Colorado, not of course on the grounds of the state constitution, which had been amended by Amendment II, but on the basis of the federal Constitution. Issue 3 in Cincinnati was held unconstitutional on virtually identical grounds by a federal district judge in Cincinnati, but that judgment was later overruled by the Court of Appeals in the Sixth Circuit. That case is now under appeal to the Supreme Court of the United States, but the Colorado case, *Romer v. Evans*, was already argued before the Court in October 1995, and a decision in that case is expected any week now. [Amendment II was struck down as unconstitutional in May 1996.] And indeed, it is the prospect of that decision, prefigured last fall in the oral argument, that sets off tremors in the land, and impels the Congress to act.

On its face, of course, that case does not strictly involve gay marriage. But the resolution of that case could have a profound effect on the way that the Full Faith and Credit clause works upon the States on the matter of gay marriage. It will come as no surprise that the opponents of Amendment II in Colorado will offer a strikingly different account of that measure from the one I have offered here. They find, in the Amendment, a provision that withholds from gays and lesbians an "equal" right to participate in the political process. But they find this subtle denial of rights without the presence of those devices that awakened our sensitivities in the past: The Amendment disfranchised no one. It offered no literacy tests or contrivances to block voters from the rolls. It removed from no person the right to run for office, contribute money or buy advertising to support any candidate or any proposition put before the voters. Judge Jeffrey Bayless noted in the county court in Denver, in December 1993, that gays and lesbians were about 4 per cent of the population of Colorado, and yet they had attracted to their side about 46 per cent of the vote on Amendment. As Bayless remarked, "that is a demonstration of power, not powerlessness."

The interests of gays

Still, it is argued that Amendment II would impair the freedom of gays to participate in politics because it would make it notably harder for them to secure legislation to advance their interests. But the interests of gays may well be protected by measures that do not pick out gays for special mention, and it has been pointed out that nothing in those protections has been diminished. The laws, say, that bar discrimination based on race would still apply to gays who suffer discrimination based on race. As Justice Antonin Scalia pointed out during the oral argument, it requires no special provision to protect gays from "gay bashing." Gays are protected here by the same laws on assault that protect, in their sweep, the "bashing" of anyone. Gays and lesbians would indeed be hampered if they sought legislation to pick out gays for a "quota preference" or "preferential treatment" (in the words of Amendment II). But they remain free to campaign and vote for the repeal of Amendment II. In the meantime, they suffer a burden here in securing legislation only in the way that other groups suffer similar burdens when a constitution has placed certain ends beyond the reach of a legislature. We need only remind ourselves that the Thirteenth Amendment had the most emphatic effect in removing, from a distinct class of persons, the possibility of securing legislation to advance or protect their interests. The holders of property in slaves suddenly found swept away all of the local laws and statutes that cast protections around their peculiar property. We cannot complain of such sweeping effects, in protecting interests, or foreclosing legislation, unless we can complain about the substance of the constitutional amendment itself.

And there, the defenders of Amendment II will suffer no strain in contending that the measure was amply justified. The Amendment licensed no regimen of criminal prosecutions directed at gays and lesbians, and indeed it would be more accurate to describe this measure as part of a policy of broader tolerance: It could be said, with more strictness, that the Amendment merely preserved for people, in their private settings, the freedom to respect their own moral and religious judgments on the matter of homosexuality. Yet, this sense of the matter seemed to elude Justices Anthony Kennedy and Sandra Day O'Connor during the oral argument, and indeed these justices seemed to suffer a certain bewilderment in grasping this Amendment in Colorado. Their evident burdens in understanding this case begat the sober reckoning that the judges were about to stumble yet again into a momentous decision, with reasoning that bore only the most infirm connection to the issues at hand.

The tea leaves suggest so far that the Court has no intention of overruling *Bowers v. Hardwick*, that notable case, in 1986, in which the Court declined to overturn the laws on sodomy in the separate States. But if the Court strikes down the Amendment in Colorado, my own reading is that the decision will be understood, in effect, as the overruling of *Bowers*, even if the Court does not care yet to acknowledge what it has done. For several years, judges at all levels in the country have shown a willingness to strike at any law that casts an adverse judgment on homosexuality, without being overly fastidious about their reasoning. Without any prodding or direction from the Supreme Court, the judges have been acting as though it were already wrong, on constitutional grounds, to take an illiberal view of gay rights. And if the Court now strikes down the Amendment in Colorado, we can count on the fact that many judges, throughout the country, will extract from that decision this principle: that it is now immanently suspect, on constitutional grounds, to plant, anywhere in the laws, a policy that casts an adverse judgment on homosexuality, or accords to homosexuality a lesser standing or legitimacy than the sexuality "imprinted in our natures."

The question of what is suitable for marriage is quite separate from the matter of love.

But any judgment of that kind, emerging from the case in Colorado, would be amplified in its importance through the workings of the Full Faith and Credit clause. Under that provision of the Constitution we typically presume that the driver's license awarded in California would be honored in Massachusetts—or that the marriage performed in Kentucky will be respected in Maine. And yet, not always: Some of these arrangements, springing from other states, may be at odds with certain moral understandings, shared within the community, and planted deeply in the laws and public policy of the state. It is taken then, as rather clear, that a state may refuse to recognize incestuous marriages. When it comes to the prospect of homosexual marriage, most states show traces of the moral concerns that would bear on this question. Many states retain their laws on sodomy; or they refuse to extend rights of adoption to couples of the same sex; or they suggest in other ways that the laws will not endorse or promote homosexuality. One way or another, then, the states would hold now a ground for refusing to credit gay marriages imported from other states. But that is exactly the prop that could be removed by a decision in the case from Colorado.

If that decision runs against the state, a federal judge, armed with that decision, could strike down anything in the laws or public policies of a state that implies an adverse judgment on homosexuality. In effect, the state could be denied the right to cast any moral judgment at all on this matter. And with that ground of objection swept away, there would be, within the laws of the state, no tenable ground for holding back and refusing to credit gay marriage.

The meaning of marriage

Of course, the "problem" here would dissolve as a problem if the understanding of marriage could simply be broadened to encompass people of the same sex. And if marriage were simply an artifact of the "positive law," if it could mean just anything the positive law proclaimed it to mean, then the positive law could define just about anything as a marriage. It could discard, as so many arbitrary vestiges of the past, the restrictions placed on the age of the married partners, or their degree of blood relation. If it were simply a matter of promulgating, through the positive law, a definition of marriage and the partners, why shouldn't it be possible to permit a mature woman, past child bearing, to marry her grown son? In fact, why would it not be possible to permit a man, much taken with himself, to marry himself? Enough people about us have already fallen into a certain kind of "dualism"—as when they tell us, for example, that they are "at ease with themselves"—so that it requires no conceptual stretch these days for a man to wed himself. The notion of a no-fault divorce later may raise stickier problems, but the marriage itself may be easier to entertain. Of course, certain sticklers for language are likely to wonder whether a "marriage" or "wedding" must not imply at least two persons. But when matters are taken back to an original ground, we may raise the question of just why the law would be justified in attaching such decisive importance to numbers: Why would it be warranted then in withholding then the blessings of marriage from a man who had not yet found a spouse?

> *We do not need a marriage to mark the presence of love, but a marriage marks something matchless in a framework for the begetting and nurturance of children.*

But even people of ordinary wit will quickly suspect that we are not dealing here merely with the conventions of our language: They may suspect, with common sense, that the notion of marriage may not be altered to fit marriage *di solo* [alone] without altering the defining logic of marriage. And in the same way, I would suggest that the notion of marriage could not be stretched to encompass people of the same sex without altering out of shape the definition that represents the coherence and meaning of marriage. The irony then for gay activists would be this: Were the notion of marriage so altered as to accommodate them, the move would set off deeper changes in the definition of marriage, and as a consequence, marriage would lose the special significance that makes it an object of such craving, right now, for many gays and lesbians.

This matter is not inscrutable or mysterious, and we can test it for ourselves with a kind of thought-experiment. First, we need to remind ourselves that what is in question, on this issue, is not the matter of love. There are relations of deep, abiding love between brothers and sisters, parents and children, grandparents and grandchildren. In the nature of things, those loves cannot be diminished as loves because they are not attended by penetration, or because they are not expressed in marriage. Nor do these people suffer an unwarranted discrimination if they are not permitted to manifest their love in a marriage.

If marriage were detached from that natural teleology of the body, on what ground of principle could the law confine marriage to "couples"?

The question of what is suitable for marriage is quite separate from the matter of love, though of course it cannot be detached from love. The love of marriage is directed to a different end, or it is woven into a different meaning, rooted in the character and ends of marriage. That character, and those ends, cannot be separated from the fact that we are, as the saying goes, "souls embodied," and that certain bodily acts must carry within themselves a significance that cannot be trivialized. The matter may be muted, but we all suspect that, one way or another, this question cannot be discussed without getting back to the "N-word" [nature]. Any discussion of sexuality must take its bearings from the meaning of sexuality in the strictest sense, which is the sexuality imprinted in our very natures—in the obdurate fact that we are all, as the saying goes, "engendered." We are, each of us, born a man or a woman. The committee needs no testimony from an expert witness to decode this point: Our engendered existence, as men and women, offers the most unmistakable, natural signs of the meaning and purpose of sexuality. And that is the function and purpose of begetting. At its core, it is hard to detach marriage from what may be called the "natural teleology of the body," namely, the inescapable fact that only two people, not three, only a man and a woman, can beget a child. We do not need a marriage to mark the presence of love, but a marriage marks something matchless in a framework for the begetting and nurturance of children. It means that a child enters the world in a framework of lawfulness, with parents who are committed to her care and nurturance for the same reason that they are committed to each other. By that we used to mean: They have foregone their freedom to be quit of these responsibilities when it suits their convenience. And even at those moments when marriages break down, this framework of law has the advantage at least of assigning responsibility for the care of children.

This is not to say, of course, that every marriage must produce children, and I'm afraid that gay activists have lured themselves into a false serenity in their conviction that a sterile couple proves the falsity of distinguishing between heterosexual and gay couples on the matter of marriage. But even people not covered over with college degrees have been able to grasp over the years the natural correspondences that establish the coherence in the design of marriage: There is a natural correspondence between the notion of marriage and the sexual coupling, the merging of bodies, in the "unitive significance" of marriage; and there is the plainest, natural connection between that act of coupling and the begetting of children. The children embody the "wedding" of the couples by combining in themselves the features of both parents. These meanings are so evident, these natural correspondences so fixed, that nothing in them is impaired if a couple happens to be incapable of begetting children. Their marital acts retain the same significance in the unitive scheme of marriage. And much the same understanding probably lies behind our surety that nothing in the significance, or the meaning, of rape is altered in the slightest degree if the female victim turns out to be sterile.

My argument, in any event, is that there is finally no getting around the fact that the meaning of marriage must be connected to that "natural teleology of the body." And if marriage is detached from that connection, it loses the defining features, in principle, that cabin its meaning and establish its coherence. This is where we could put more precisely that thought-experiment I suggested, and we would put it through these questions: If marriage were detached from that natural teleology of the body, *on what ground of principle could the law confine marriage to "couples"?* If the law permitted the marriage of people of the same sex, what is the ground of principle then on which the law would rule out as illegitimate the people who profess that their own love is not confined to a coupling of two, but connected in a larger cluster of three or four? The confining of marriage to two may stand out then as nothing more than the most arbitrary fixation on numbers. But if that arrangement of plural partners were permitted to people of the same sex, how could it be denied in principle to ensembles of mixed sexes? That is to say, we would be back, in principle, to the acceptance of polygamy. And while we are at it, we might ask how the law, on these new premises, rules out marriage between parents and their grown children.

Clearly, the right to gay marriage cannot be found in the text of the Constitution.

The point is easily and often mistaken, and so I would underscore the fact that I am not offering here a prediction, or invoking a "parade of horribles." I am not predicting that, if gay marriage were allowed, we would be engulfed by incest and polygamy. What is being posed here is a question of principle: What is the ground on which the law would turn back these challenges? It cannot be, "That isn't what we do here," for that answer would suffice right now about same-sex marriage. And again, I do not expect that many people will be pressing, at least initially, for polygamy or even more exotic forms of "marriage." More than that, I will not suppose that our colleagues on the opposite side of this issue have even a remote interest in promoting polygamy or incest. But one thing can be attributed to the gay activists quite fairly and accurately and that is that they do have the most profound interest, rooted in the logic of their doctrine, in discrediting the notion that marriage finds its defining ground in "nature." Their rhetorical strategy, their public arguments, have all been directed explicitly to the derision of that claim that sexuality in the strictest sense involves the sexuality "imprinted in our natures." And for that reason, we can count on the fact that there will be someone, somewhere, ready to press this issue to the next level by raising a challenge in the court and testing the limits even further.

The argument for gay rights has been that nature is indeed more malleable than we have supposed, more open to reshaping or deconstruction, in the culture. In this construction, marriage does become a matter solely of convention and opinion, and therefore it can be given virtually any shape by the positive law. Under those conditions, there would be no ground on which to reject, in principle, any of the more exotic possibilities I have suggested here as potential new marriages. The gay activists do not intend, I am sure, to bring back polygamy or introduce novelties even stranger. But they show a willingness to break down the barriers of principle and even they may not grasp the fuller sweep of the changes they are triggering.

The Supreme Court and the Constitution

Yet, apart from these notable problems, it seems not to have occurred to the proponents of gay marriage that, in the sweep of their argument, they have moved decisively away from the ground marked off by the Supreme Court as the only ground on which judges may vindicate rights of "privacy" and sexual freedom. In this field, everything seems to begin with *Griswold v. Connecticut*, dealing with contraception and marital privacy. At the end of his opinion for the Court, Justice William O. Douglas sought to reinforce his argument that the Court was dealing here with a freedom that did not depend on the positive law, because it was older than the law, and perhaps even antecedent to civil society:

> We deal with a right of privacy older than the Bill of Rights—older than our political parties, older than our school system. Marriage is a combining together for better or for worse, hopefully enduring, and intimate to the degree of being sacred.

The Court claimed the authority, in *Griswold*, to override the policy enacted by elected officials in Connecticut, even though the Court could not cite any right of marital privacy mentioned in the text of the Constitution. Douglas's argument has been taken to suggest that he and his colleagues were appealing then to a freedom that did not depend on the positive law, even the positive law of the Constitution. He was appealing to a notion of rights that ran quite beyond the positive law itself, because they were in some sense antecedent to civil society and "older than the

Bill of Rights" because they were older than the Constitution itself. The language was foreign to judges appointed to the Court in the era of the New Deal, but Douglas was invoking all of the properties of an argument grounded in "natural right." He seemed to be appealing, that is, to "nature" and a ground of right that would justify judges in overturning the judgments made by majorities in legislatures.

But if we are to take the word of gay activists and the advocates of gay marriage, there is not the slightest claim that the rights they seek are grounded in nature. In fact, that notion is quite explicitly disclaimed and ridiculed. Yet, if they turn away from that ground of argument, what exactly would be the ground on which judges invoke the Constitution to overturn policies like Amendment II in Colorado? Clearly, the right to gay marriage cannot be found in the text of the Constitution, and it is even clearer that it cannot be found in the "traditions" that have informed our laws. By their own word, the gay activists insist that the ground of rights is not to be found in "natural law" but convention or positive law. And those who would live by the positive law should suffer the implications: If there are no moral truths grounded in nature—if all moral truths depend on local opinion and positive law—then the only test of Amendment II or the Defense of Marriage Act is whether those policies can claim the support of the majority. In the case of the Defense of Marriage Act, we can simply get on with the vote.

A cultural crisis

Still, some of us think that the positive law must be measured and justified by a more demanding standard, and so we would fill in the reasons that would justify this new bill. The Defense of Marriage Act has been brought forth to deal with a crisis running deep in our culture and jurisprudence, and it has sought to engage that crisis in the most modest and economical way. The crisis in our culture involves an erosion of the traditional understandings that have enveloped sexuality, the family, and indeed life itself, in the sense of creating new franchises for the destruction of life in the name of "personal autonomy." To be more strictly accurate, we have a campaign waged to transform the culture through the law, or through the control of the courts. The new ethic of "autonomy" goes along with a new detachment from the moral tradition on the matter of sex and the family. That new ethic finds its main centers of support in the federal judiciary, and among the class that controls the leading universities and major media. As a class the members show a remarkable leaning toward the most expansive, unqualified right to abortion, to assisted suicide, to gay rights. The surveys persistently reveal a profile of opinion that sets this political class apart from the opinions that prevail among most other Americans. And that may suggest, precisely, why this program of cultural change cannot be accomplished through legislatures and elections. No voting public in this country has ever voted to install abortion on demand at every stage of the pregnancy, and it is hard to imagine a scheme of same-sex marriage voted in by the public in a referendum. These things must be imposed by the courts, if they are to be imposed at all, and that concert to impose them has been evident, on gay rights, over the last few years. In this respect, it became hard to ignore the trend marked by *Romer v. Evans* and *Equality Foundation of Cincinnati v. City of Cincinnati:* A college of judges has evidently been busy at work advancing an agenda for the rest of us, and giving Providence a helping hand.

The Defense of Marriage Act

In the presence of this movement, this flexing of judicial power, the Defense of Marriage Act represents the most restrained and modulated effort to meet the crisis. It engages that crisis by forcing a debate on the central question: the moral ground of marriage, and the meaning of sexuality. The Act offers a response on that issue; it offers a counter to the movement of the federal judges; it invites a debate on the main question. And yet it does not overreach: It does not touch the full range of authorities that Congress can invoke—and it touches nothing more than it strictly needs to touch in addressing these issues right now. The Congress does not invoke its authority under the Fourteenth Amendment to contest the issue of marriage in the separate states. Instead, it leaves the states free to settle their own policy on gay marriage. If Hawaii proceeds to authorize marriage for couples of the same sex, the Congress would not threaten to disturb that judgment. The Congress chooses to engage the question only by engaging the instruments, or authorities, that must fall clearly within the reach of the national government.

> *It surely cannot be a novelty to make explicit what has ever been our tradition, that marriage "means only a legal union between one man and one woman as husband and wife."*

It must be taken as an argument freighted with irony, if not an outright jest, that the opponents of this bill have railed against the move to "federalize" the issue of marriage. It surely cannot represent a stretching of the federal authority for the Congress simply to address the meaning that attaches to the notion of "marriage" wherever that term is used in the federal code. Apart from that, it is the Full Faith and Credit clause, a clause of the federal Constitution, that promises to act now as the engine that spreads same-sex marriage from Hawaii to other states. The problem would not be with us were it not for that clause in the Constitution. Nor would the "promise" for gays: The gay activists who have been promoting the litigation in Hawaii, or indeed charters to Hawaii, have been weaving into their plans the operation of the Full Faith and Credit clause. It must be counted as political theater when the same activists profess surprise and outrage now that anyone should "federalize" this issue. Plainly, the Full Faith and Credit clause is central to the scheme of amplifying gay rights; and if Congress may not legislate under this federal clause, what other institution could possibly claim the authority to legislate?

I have heard it remarked, in complaint, that this legislation, defining marriage in a federal statute, is "unprecedented," and I find myself straining to discover what that could possibly mean. It surely cannot be a novelty to make explicit what has ever been our tradition, that marriage "means only a legal union between one man and one woman as husband and wife." That cannot be the earth-shaking novelty here. The legislation is unprecedented only in the sense that, since the days of polygamy in Nevada, the point never seemed to be in need of stating. That is, since 1993 or 1994. What is novel, again, is not the point that the Congress is restating, but the need even to restate it. In the curious inversion that seems characteristic mainly of our own time, the act of restating, the act of confirming the tradition, is itself taken as an "irregular" or radical move. That we should summon the nerve simply to restate the traditional understanding is taken as nothing less than an act of aggression. Apparently, the public is meant to be put into a condition in which it will accept the remodelling of our laws that the courts have been quietly, and discreetly, arranging—and accept all of this without making a scene.

15

Same-Sex Marriage Would Harm Society

Burman Skrable

Burman Skrable is a freelance writer and quality control officer for the Unemployment Insurance Service's Division of Program and Review in the U.S. Department of Labor.

Children are vital to the future stability of society. Society encourages the formation of marriages in order to ensure that enough children are born and that these children are properly raised. The sexual revolution—which broke the bonds between marriage, sex, and children—has weakened the institution of marriage and has led to widespread acceptance of homosexuality. Legalizing same-sex marriage would further erode marriage and would legitimize homosexual behavior.

This season's [1996] hot topic, spurred by the pending case before the Supreme Court of Hawaii and now the U.S. Supreme Court's *Romer v. Evans* decision [which struck down Colorado's Amendment 2, which prohibited local governments from passing laws to specifically protect gays and lesbians from discrimination], is same-sex or "gay" marriage. Editorials in the mainstream secular press have favored it nearly overwhelmingly, even though it is without precedent in any civilized society.

Two columns in 1996 in the *Northern Virginia Journal* newspapers by Karen Murray illustrate the tack taken by columnists beating the drum for this latest development of the sexual revolution. In both, Ms. Murray asks a good question: "What does marriage have to fear" from same-sex marriage? Her answer is, not surprisingly, "nothing." To Murray, same-sex marriage is a simple issue of justice to gays, will promote a more stable lifestyle among gays, and will redound to the advantage of any children being raised in gay households. (The same argument was made in the "Doonesbury" cartoon.) Its benefits seem so obvious to her that she cannot conceive of a real argument that the institution of marriage will be affected. Of course, right-wingers (to Murray, who else would question gay marriage?) can raise either of two kinds of invalid or pretend arguments.

From Burman Skrable, "Homosexual Marriage: Much to Fear," *Culture Wars*, October 1996. Reprinted with permission of *Culture Wars*, 206 Marquette Ave., South Bend, IN 46617.

People who have "Talked to God" either directly or indirectly can make sincere arguments on religious grounds, but these are *ipso facto* inadmissible in our secularized political environment. Then there are insincere smokescreens by homophobes and other people who think gays are "weird." That's it. Case dismissed.

Valid arguments against gay marriage

I'd like to suggest that Murray's short list is a bit too short; there definitely is a valid argument, and Christians, especially Catholics, should be making it regularly. Right now, it is hard to reduce it to a neat 15-second soundbite, but perhaps even that may come with time. Unfortunately, most current arguments made by Christians are religious statements which seem to play to her hand; they are more statements of authority or belief than arguments totally based on fact. A good example is a recent statement by Archbishop James Stafford of Denver. He praised normal marriage as "the foundation of civilization for the past 1500 years" and noted that people "have read reality through its nuptial/marital/covenantal meaning." Promoting homosexual activity "as a valid moral option" directly assaults "the ancient moral vision which, for more than 15 centuries, has established the private and public responsibilities indispensable for the free order of society." What he said is true and inspiring, but would make not the slightest dent in the consciousness of someone like Murray, unless it should cause her to wonder why, if same-sex "marriage" is such an undiluted blessing, it has been overlooked for all of recorded history.

> *The traditional family—husband, wife, and natural children—is the only way societies have ever found of providing well for stability in the present and for our future.*

In defense of the archbishop and other Christians who have tried to respond to the demand for same-sex marriage from their religious beliefs, it should he noted that this is not the first time an institution or doctrine which has been unquestioningly accepted for aeons is suddenly challenged, and whose defenders found themselves grasping, at first ineffectively, for an appropriate response. In fact, history is full of similar instances, although our era may be the most "challenged." We live in an age which can almost be defined by its proclivity for questioning practically every received doctrine and belief, and by the way our dominant attitude-shaping institutions have shifted the benefit of the doubt from the defenders of the status quo to its challengers. This shift in the burden of proof has undoubtedly helped ensure the success of the sexual revolution, which has systematically challenged the rationale for one thing connected with sex after another. That said, however, it is definitely high time, if not too late, to catch up with the need for an effective response. Much rides on it.

We need to move the foundation of our argument from the religious to the scientific. The validity of many of the tenets of our Christian beliefs have been well proved by the social sciences. Thus, there is nothing particularly religious about the argument I propose. Its main premise is that societies have a life-and-death interest in ensuring their own survival, and thus a responsibility to act to further that interest. The importance of this approach was acknowledged, although not developed, by Cardinal Bernard Law. Queried by the *National Catholic Register* in Portland, Oregon, about the Hawaii case, the cardinal said "The issue is—what is marriage? What's the State's interest in marriage?" *(Register,* July 7, 1996).

This viewpoint attempts to develop just this line of thinking. It is structured as follows. First, one must consider why societies recognize marriage in the first place. This involves specifying certain needs which societies have, which societies consider to be satisfied by marriage. Second, having identified the needs, we must consider what characteristics marriage should have to fulfill that role. Third, we consider how extending the privilege of marriage to same-sex couples would affect the ability of marriage to do what societies need it to do.

Society's needs

To remain vital, every society must ensure stability in the present and provide for its future. Everyone, including the homosexually oriented, depends on these things being done, and done well. The two objectives are closely related, and children are at the focus of both. Providing for the future means bearing, educating and socializing children; children are our social security, economically, physically and emotionally. If there are not enough of them, there will eventually be a disproportion between those able to work and those who cannot, and the burden of supporting the dependent population can become so severe that it strains society's bonds. (See: "Contracepting Social Security" by W. Patrick Cunningham, *Culture Wars,* July/August 1996.) If the children are not raised properly, the well-being of those who depend on them later is threatened as much as, if not more than, if there are too few children.

Marriage provides for society's future by formally constituting the family. The traditional family—husband, wife, and natural children—is the only way societies have ever found of providing well for stability in the present and for our future. The family is the first community, the original unit which precedes and forms the basis of all larger and subsequent units. It is the original school for children, where they are taught all the values and mores that form them in how they interact, first with one another, and later with others to whom they are not related. It is irreplaceable in that it is a community of love, a community based on love; what parents do for children out of love cannot be replicated in a setting where the same tasks are done for pay.

As all who have undertaken the task of raising a family—and those who merely observe with detachment—will agree, it is an awesome and difficult business. For a couple to bear and raise children, and often even to stay together, is hard work and expensive. In its own interest, society must do what it can to ease those burdens and reward what is so central to its stability and continuation. By easing some of the financial burden and elevating the stature of the family, society hopes to induce its citizens to follow in the footsteps of their parents and grandparents and form families.

Marriage can thus be seen as a formal institution structured by society to help it meet its needs for stability in the present and continued existence over time. In marriage, a couple makes a formal, public commitment to one another to live as a single unit; the community endorses and ratifies that commitment. It also extends special recognition and usually various financial privileges to couples making this commitment. Its reason for doing so, as noted above, is its expectation that the couple will form a family unit, to bear and raise properly the children the society needs. Society's interest in all this is the children, period. Aside from the expectation of childbearing and child raising, it has no strong interest in making marriage a privileged institution.

It should be noted that society recognizes marriage in *two* ways: legally and morally. Both have positive and negative aspects. Legally, society may give marriage positive stature by granting financial benefits such as tax reductions, rights of inheritance, etc., to married couples. The community may also legally prohibit activities considered to weaken marriage or the family—passing laws prohibiting or restricting divorce, adultery, sodomy, contraception, renting to cohabiting couples, etc. Extralegally or morally, society grants its approval and recognition to married couples by establishing a climate favorable to the institution; and it also provides social disapproval of things destructive of marriage and family life even when not legally proscribed. The legal and the moral obviously influence one another. Ideas have consequences, one of which is their embodiment in law; and law is a great teacher and shaper of attitudes.

The kind of marriage society needs

The traditional understanding of marriage, and of the family that results from it, lines up perfectly to provide for the key needs identified above. Marriage once meant a permanent bond, the only approved locus for sex (i.e., marriage both establishes an exclusive sexual relationship and only the marriage relationship legitimizes sexual activity), and children. It went without saying that it was a man-woman relationship. Males and females have a natural complementarity in the process not only of procreating but also of raising children, and children thrive in an atmosphere of stability and commitment. Children also need the role models of both father and mother for their complete development. The atmosphere of stable commitment also helps regulate all of society's rhythms.

What marriage has become

One would hardly recognize in today's marriage the institution which the previous section argues best meets society's needs for stability and continuation. The villain of the piece is the generations-old social experiment called the sexual revolution. It has gradually drained the content from marriage, and with it, the vitality of the family. The main thrust of the sexual revolution has been to enable adults to separate sex from children and relieve them of binding commitments to one another. I'm not enough of an historian to know which came first: trying to chicken out on our lifetime commitments to one another, or separating the egg from the sperm. Whatever the order, the sexual revolution attacked, and gradually weakened, the covalent bonds of the marriage-sex-children triad. No-fault divorce vitiated permanence; first contraception and then abortion made the connection between sex and children optional; respected marriage gurus touted "open marriage." With sex no longer meaning children, the institutional warrant for marriage was questionable, and hence the fashionability of "living together."

Allowing homosexual marriage would further dilute the uniqueness of marriage by opening it to all who want it, regardless of their potential to fulfill an essential societal function.

The sexual revolution attacked both the legal framework surrounding and protecting marriage and the family and the moral climate. On the legal front, Supreme Court decisions overturned laws against contraception and abortion, states liberalized laws regulating divorce, and various laws affecting homosexual behavior have been challenged. In addition, there is a movement to establish a "right" of open homosexuality. Morally, the legal climate, technology and media-led opinion have all greatly influenced society's approvals and disapprovals. Living together and voluntary single parenthood receive hardly a blink today, whereas families with more than two children can expect many arched eyebrows and the obligatory query "don't you know about birth control?"

The result is, I would argue, that at present we're not doing well at providing for the future or ensuring stability. Birthrates are barely at replacement level, and fewer and fewer of the children born are being socialized well. Crime, especially violent crime, has been rising and some analysts, such as Princeton Professor John DiIulio, say the worst is yet to come. The reason is the breakdown of marriage and the traditional family. The evidence relating deviations from the traditional family structure to problems for children is flooding in. Children raised by single parents and the children of divorce don't do as well in school as their counterparts raised in traditional two-parent families, and have more behavioral problems. They are more prone to criminal behavior, to premarital sex and abortions, and to divorce if they do marry.

Homosexual "marriage"?

The sexual revolution gradually brought us to the point where the complex fabric of laws and mores which together supported and sustained marriage and the family has largely been unravelled. We are beginning to see the effects on social behavior. More to the point, these changes have gradually eroded our understanding of what marriage is. No longer is marriage considered universally in the public mind as a permanent union; no longer is it considered to have any necessary connection to children; no longer does it universally bind to fidelity; and that sex should be reserved for it is today's unthinkable thought. Marriage has become a mere diaphanous thing. To Murray, for example, it means a public declaration of "the mutual devotion between any pair of adults," a pledge of "support, loyalty protection of the partner's privacy" which "others are expected to honor and reinforce."

The evolutionary emptying of the concept of marriage, and the concomitant acceptance of homosexual relations—both products of the same revolutionary forces—largely explain the drive for homosexual "marriage." Who, homosexual or heterosexual, could conceive of same-sex "marriage" if marriage meant more than it does today? More than anything else, our increasing technical ability to sever the biological link between sex and children, and the contraceptive mentality that grew from it—the belief that to separate sex from its natural consequences was not only natural but a right—probably paved the way for tolerating homosexual relations. But tolerance is not the same thing as acceptance. And even though marriage may now be but a shadow of its former self, it still retains some power to make sexual activity legitimate. So, same-sex couples grasp at it even when so many heterosexual couples find it superfluous. They may not believe society needs the institution of marriage, but it would salve their consciences and help them hold their heads high in public.

Same-sex marriage would really represent a drop to a new societal or moral low, because it would represent society's formal endorsement of homosexual activity.

In view of the foregoing, it is easier to see what extending marriage to same-sex couples would do to the institution of marriage.

1) It would remove marriage's sole original defining characteristic, that it is a union of one man and one woman.

2) Although it would not change much of what is left of marriage—because not much is left today—it would lock in the 'gains' of the sexual revolution. That, by itself, is extremely serious: what society really needs is the restoration of marriage; same-sex marriage would continue marriage on its present search for the bottom. That would further solidify the notions that sex need not have a necessary connection to procreation, nor marriage to children. Similarly, it is hard to imagine that same-sex couples—especially males—would want to see marriage restored to being a permanent and exclusive union. Male homosexual relations are inherently so transitory that many gay activists opposed same-sex marriage on the grounds that it would be so restrictive of the gay lifestyle that failure would be virtually guaranteed. In short, marriage would be further solidified as a meaningless institution in which society has no inherent interest, unless one makes the leap (not uncommonly implied today) of saying that society's real interest is in making us all feel good by legitimating every conceivable choice.

Allowing homosexual marriage would further dilute the uniqueness of marriage by opening it to all who want it, regardless of their potential to fulfill an essential societal function. If a privilege is open to all, it is no longer a privilege. This great levelling process would further diminish the incentives to bear and raise children. Homosexual marriage is a chimera of the real thing on which society depends for its continuation and health. It would further reinforce the sexual revolution's notion—which is too strong already—that any connection between sex and children is purely optional. It sends the subliminal message that everything should be a matter of choice, that nothing is a given or need be permanent, and that sexual differences are imaginative fictions imposed through socialization. I believe that these effects are enough to fear from extending marriage to same-sex couples.

Although most of its proponents are reticent to elaborate on this, same-sex marriage would really represent a drop to a new societal or moral low, because it would represent society's formal endorsement of homosexual activity. By giving it the writ of marriage, society gives it the stamp of approval. As Alexander Pope said of vice, "We first endure, then pity, then embrace." With homosexual activity, we are now probably somewhere between enduring and pitying; same-sex marriage would be the embrace. Thus would society endorse an activity which its true interest is in eliminating. The hazards to the public health which homosexual sex represents, from HIV infections on down, are well known. Same-sex marriage would only raise them.

Those who advocate homosexual marriage often make some related assertions that deserve commentary:

Assertion One: Homosexual marriage wouldn't increase the number of gay kids. Really? Homosexual marriage will—as I believe its advocates intend—boost the acceptability of homosexual relations, which has to raise experimentation. Experimentation among the sexually confused, as many teens are, leads to many becoming locked in to behavior patterns, in this case, homosexual ones. By blessing and legitimizing homosexual behavior, same-sex marriage would tend to endorse and promote such behavior across the board. What, pray tell, is society's interest in doing that?

Homosexual unions are rarely about begetting children and only slightly more often involve raising them.

Assertion Two: Not allowing homosexuals to marry worsens the lot of kids being raised in same-sex households. On this, two points. First, we don't know the long-term effects of child raising in same-sex households. At present, it has the status of an underground social experiment. If its anything like the single-parent model—and I believe it is—its something I don't think we want to endorse, period. Second, and in general, bringing in kids to this discussion is largely a red herring, the kind of hard case that makes for bad law. If there's one thing the sexual revolution hasn't been about, its the interests of children. Its *raison d'etre* has been the separation of sexual activity from its inconvenient biological consequences by actions taken before, during, or after (often much after) sex. Homosexual unions are rarely about begetting children and only slightly more often involve raising them. We need to get real on this.

Assertion Three: Allowing homosexuals to marry would add some stability to the gay scene. Well, maybe. But as I argue above, we're talking about '90s marriage, the kind that uplifts without restricting. It's a marriage contract with the freeing codicils: Open marriage with no-fault divorce if things don't work out. This is all we expect of heterosexual aspirants. Wouldn't it be discriminatory to expect more of gays and lesbians? From what I've read about the dynamic of homosexual relations, I find it impossible to believe homosexuals as a group would give up, or be able to give up, their lifestyle. Nor can I imagine they would be willing to make a commitment to premarital celibacy for the sake of the right to marry. The notion of same-sex marriage, as I understand it, is "marriage and . . ."—marriage in addition to the sexual freedoms they now enjoy. And, assuming for the sake of argument that marriage would act as a noticeable brake on homosexual promiscuity, is that a worthwhile tradeoff against the overall damage to society from continuing marriage on its downward trajectory and from giving a boost to homosexual activity?

Presumptively fertile couples who marry but . . . do not intend to have children, are insidious enemies of marriage.

Assertion Four: But society already allows heterosexual couples to marry who cannot procreate or who have no intention of procreating, so why not same-sex couples? This point is perhaps the most difficult to deal with. The latter group, presumptively fertile couples who marry but (without any serious medical or financial reason) do not intend to have children, are insidious enemies of marriage. With their decisions to make childbearing optional they have come into marriage as a fifth column to prepare the way for homosexual marriage. They are the free-riders upon the institution, taking the privileges without the burdens. Murray is nearly right to suggest that society has no more interest in granting them a privileged position than it does homosexual couples. Unfortunately, society has little choice but to continue to allow them to marry, giving them the benefit of the doubt that they may eventually have children. They illustrate how sufficient abuse of freedom can destroy any institution.

The harder case advocates of same-sex marriage raise is couples known, or likely, to be infertile—couples beyond their childbearing years or those with various handicaps rendering them infertile. What's the difference between allowing them to marry and allowing same-sex couples to marry? Isn't the only societal interest involved the more limited one that the union will contribute to the general stability of the community by enhancing the couple's happiness and limiting promiscuity?

The answer is that the two cases differ in at least three major ways. One is the inherently different orientation of the two kinds of unions toward parenthood noted above. Infertile heterosexual couples, including those beyond their childbearing years, still value children and want to make their unions a sacrifice for raising them. "Physical sterility in fact can be for spouses the occasion for other important services to the life of the human person, for example adoption, various forms of educational work, and assistance to other families and to poor or handicapped children" *(Familiaris Consortio, 14).* Couples beyond their childbearing years often are raising children from previous marriages and grandchildren. Same-sex unions lack this essential orientation toward both physical and spiritual parentage. Second, even among the relatively few same-sex couples motivated by a desire to raise children, there is a difference of role models. Having two moms or two dads is not the same as one parent of each sex. Third, allowing same-sex marriage says many things about what marriage is and what it means that go well beyond the notion of couples whose main likeness is that none of them can produce children. Restricting marriage to heterosexual couples continues to say that marriage is oriented toward procreation, and that sex is a social act oriented toward procreation and not merely a private rite of the couple.

There are reasons against gay marriage

This viewpoint has been an attempt to show that there is a very real sociological argument against same-sex marriage that is neither religious nor a front for aversion to persons with homosexual attractions. There are serious public policy reasons for not only keeping marriage heterosexual as it is, but also for attempting to restore its former meaning. Homosexual marriage would further weaken an already-damaged institution, to the detriment of us all—homosexuals included.

I also have tried to show that the push for homosexual marriage, while serious, is best understood as a symptom of a larger and more serious problem with our understanding of sex and marriage. The underlying causes of this serious problem are deeply rooted within our collective consciousness, and involve the acceptance—often by many profamily stalwarts themselves—of the destructive premises of the sexual revolution. Rooting these premises will be anything but easy; for many, no legislative or judicial remedy is possible. Profamily groups are right to fight homosexual marriage, however; although it may be largely symptomatic, permitting it will only make things worse.

Finally, while the argument here is explicitly nonreligious, Catholics and other Christians should see that there is no inconsistency between the underlying tenets of their faith and good public policy. A useful thought experiment is to ponder whether, and how, society's overall health and stability are improved by giving up portions of Catholic teaching on marriage and the family. We've seen many aspects of our beliefs rejected as society has "advanced": the permanence of marriage, the evils of contraception, abortion and sodomy. Now we are being enjoined to jettison the "discriminatory notion" that marriage ought to be limited to one man and one woman as the latest advance. If each of our beliefs has truly limited society's progress toward greater happiness, we should see life getting better and better, and people getting healthier and happier, with the elimination of each. Where is the evidence? The promised benefits, like the horizon, remain ahead of us, out of our grasp.

In the Catholic world-view, as I understand it, there is of course much more to marriage than its benefits to society's continuation and stability. St. Paul tells us that marriage is the concrete sign of the union between Christ the bridegroom and his bride, the Church. Theology also tells us that is also a sign of the Trinity itself—a union of two persons forming a new entity which, through the covenanted love of husband and wife, enables the creation of a third person. These theological realities say to me that marriage cannot be anything else than a union of man and woman.

They also say that the traditional marriage—permanent, heterosexual, life-giving—is the only true sacramental sign of those invisible realities whose existence must be proclaimed continually in the world. It is not in any way surprising to me, therefore, that notions of marriage which deviate from marriage in its totality will be inconsistent with the proper order, if not the very existence, of society. But that is, as the saying goes, a topic for another essay.

16

Same-Sex Marriage Would Harm Children

David Zweibel

David Zweibel is the general counsel for and director of government affairs for Agudath Israel of America, a national Orthodox Jewish organization.

Throughout history, marriage has always been the union of a man and a woman for the purpose of conceiving and raising children. It is society's responsibility to do everything it can to protect its children by strengthening the institution of marriage. Legitimizing same-sex marriage would harm children by weakening the visible link between marriage and children. Congress has the right and the authority to protect children and the integrity of marriage by denying marital status to same-sex couples.

Editor's note: The following viewpoint was originally delivered as testimony during congressional hearings on the Defense of Marriage on July 11, 1996.

In the interest of full disclosure, I should mention right up front that Agudath Israel's perspective on homosexual conduct is informed by the biblical description of such conduct as *"to'eivah"*—an abomination. *(Leviticus 20:13.)* Our perspective on civil recognition of same-sex marriage is further informed by the talmudic dictum that the nations of the world have always faithfully adhered to three basic commitments they made to G-d, one of them being *"she'ein kosvin kesuba le'zecharim"*—that they do not recognize any formal marital relationship between males. *(Hulin 92.)* For those who would exclude religious groups from the arena of public policy debate on issues where their views are shaped by religious teachings, please be advised that for Agudath Israel and its constituency, this is one such issue—as it is, no doubt, for millions of Americans of all faiths.

Happily, though, our nation in recent years has come increasingly to the recognition that religiously-grounded viewpoints do have a place at the public policy table; that constitutionally mandated neutrality toward religion does not require hostility or indifference toward religious values;

From David Zweibel, testimony before the Senate Committee on the Judiciary, July 11, 1996.

that our national dialogue on issues of profound social and moral import would be immeasurably impoverished were our churches, mosques and synagogues frozen out of the discussion. *Leviticus* is not irrelevant.

Neither is history. Marriage has existed since time immemorial, and it has always meant the sanctioned union of man and woman. Proponents of same-sex marriages seek to change not only statutory law, but also the very nature of a social institution that throughout the millennia has proven its worth as an agent of social stability and historical continuity. The title of the bill before you today, the "Defense of Marriage Act," [S. 1740] may be dramatic—but it is apt.

The bill has two substantive components. Let me review each one briefly.

Section 2 of S. 1740 would allow states not to "give effect to any public act, record, or judicial proceeding" of any sister jurisdiction concerning "a relationship between persons of the same sex that is treated as a marriage" by the sister jurisdiction.

Legalizing same-sex marriages . . . would obscure further still the vital link between marriage and children.

This provision is designed to address a threat that looms on the immediate horizon. In *Baehr v. Lewin* 852 P.2d 44 (1993), the Supreme Court of Hawaii ruled that the denial of marriage licenses to same-sex couples implicated the Hawaii state constitution's mandate that "[n]o person . . . be denied the enjoyment of the person's civil rights or be discriminated against in the exercise thereof because of . . . sex." The court further ruled that such denial may be justified only if Hawaii can demonstrate that its anti-same-sex-marriage policy advances compelling state interests and is narrowly drawn to serve those interests. The case was remanded to the lower court for a determination on the issue of compelling state interest, and the trial of that issue is scheduled to begin shortly. Many legal observers anticipate that the eventual outcome of *Baehr* will be that same-sex marriages will be recognized in Hawaii. [The court found in December 1996 that prohibiting same-sex couples to marry is discriminatory. The state has appealed the ruling to the Hawaii Supreme Court.] If so, the possibility looms large that same-sex couples from across the United States will journey to Hawaii to solemnize their "marital vows"; validate their marriage through a formal Hawaii state proceeding; and then call upon their states of domicile to accord "full faith and credit" to the Hawaii proceeding.

To use the constitutional doctrine of full faith and credit to allow the courts of Hawaii, interpreting their own state constitution, effectively to determine that the 49 other states must also recognize the validity of same-sex marriages, would be to provoke a constitutional crisis of considerable magnitude. Section 2 is designed to head off such a crisis by allowing each state to decide the matter on its own.

It is often said, correctly, that the judiciary plays a vital role in protecting the minority against the tyranny of the majority. But tyranny is by no means within the exclusive domain of the majority. An empowered minority is capable of tyranny as well—as when, for example, a court radically redefines the institution of marriage by interpreting its state constitution in a manner that is at variance with the intent of the democratically elected representatives of the people, without the benefit of public debate, without the input of public hearings, without the legitimacy of public support. The tyranny of the minority is compounded 49 times over, however, if the powerful engine of the full faith and credit doctrine is then employed to convert one state court's radicalism into the de facto law of the entire land.

Section 2 is thus a particularly appropriate exercise of Congress' constitutional authority, pursuant to Article IV, Section I, to "prescribe . . . the Effect" of one state's legal judgments on the others. *See generally* Douglas Laycock, *Equal Citizens of Equal and Territorial States: The Constitutional Foundations of Choice of Law,* 92 Colum. L. Rev. 249, 301(1992).

As noted, section 2 of the bill takes no substantive position on the validity of same-sex marriages; it allows each state to decide for itself whether to recognize such marriages that have been performed with legal sanction in other states. Section 3, in contrast, takes an affirmative stance. It declares that for purposes of federal law, notwithstanding what any individual state—or for that matter, all the states—may choose to do, the terms "marriage" and "spouse" shall not encompass same-sex unions.

The need for this legislation is manifest. The general presumption is that "federal courts should look to state law in defining terms describing familial relations." *Spearman v. Spearman,* 482 F.2d 1203, 1204 (5th Cir. 1973). If, therefore, Hawaii or any other state accords recognition to same-sex marriages, a federal court might well conclude that the various benefits federal law assigns to married couples must be made available to the same-sex couples whose "marriages" have been validated pursuant to state law. Section 3 would preclude this result by clarifying that the intent of federal law is *not* to yield to any state definition of marriage that encompasses same-sex unions.

Congress' authority to issue this definitional clarification is a simple matter of federalism. It is the federal lawmaking body, not the state courts or legislatures, that has the power to decide the meaning of terms used in federal law. Section 3 is thus an unassailable expression of congressional authority in our federal system.

The social importance of this legislation

The movement to confer the status of "marriage" upon same-sex unions is, in Agudath Israel's view, an extremely dangerous one for American society. I will focus on the two aspects of this movement that we believe should be cause for particular concern.

First, there is the question of society's attitude toward the institution of marriage itself. It has become manifestly and tragically clear in recent years that the decline of marriage has engendered enormous social costs—and, more specifically, that failure to view marriage as the cornerstone of family life has had devastating impact on children. In its 1992 report to the nation, *Beyond Rhetoric: A New American Agenda for Children and Families,* the National Commission on Children noted (at page 253) as follows:

When parents divorce or fail to marry, children are often the victims. Children who live with only one parent, usually their mothers, are six times as likely to be poor as children who live with both parents. They also suffer more emotional, behavioral, and intellectual problems. They are at greater risk of dropping out of school, alcohol and drug use, adolescent pregnancy and childbearing, juvenile delinquency, mental illness, and suicide.

It is, or ought to be, an urgent objective of public policy not only to strengthen the institution of marriage, but to do so in a manner that promotes a sense of responsibility to children. The historical genius of marriage is not merely that it constitutes the legal union of man and woman, but that it furnishes the foundation of family. Sadly, we sometimes lose sight of that reality.

Legalizing same-sex marriages—which, by biological definition, can never have anything to do with procreation—would obscure further still the vital link between marriage and children. It would convey the message that childbearing, and childrearing, are matters entirely distinct from marriage. The message is subtle, but devastating.

Second, there is the question of society's attitude toward homosexuality. As many jurisprudential scholars have noted, and as many parents and teachers instinctively recognize, government is not a neutral actor in the field of moral values; the laws by which a society chooses to govern itself have (among other things) an educational function. Conferring society's blessing upon same-sex unions by according them the legal and social status of "marriage," as Hawaii appears about to do, would convey an unmistakable imprimatur of acceptability and legitimacy upon the practice of homosexuality.

Which brings us full circle. For better or for worse, millions of Americans, of all faiths, reject the notion that homosexual conduct is merely an "alternative lifestyle," no more objectionable and no less acceptable than the traditional heterosexual lifestyle. These Americans strive hard to raise their children to recognize that not all expressions of sexuality are morally equivalent. Extending legal recognition to same-sex unions is government's way of telling those children that their parents are wrong, that their priests, ministers and rabbis are wrong, that civilized societies throughout the millennia have been wrong. We respectfully submit that government has no business conveying that message.

Agudath Israel accordingly supports the Defense of Marriage Act.

Organizations to Contact

The editors have compiled the following list of organizations concerned with the issues debated in this book. The descriptions are derived from materials provided by the organizations. All have publications or information available for interested readers. The list was compiled on the date of publication of the present volume; names, addresses, phone and fax numbers, and e-mail and Internet addresses may change. Be aware that many organizations take several weeks or longer to respond to inquiries, so allow as much time as possible.

American Civil Liberties Union (ACLU)
Lesbian and Gay Rights/AIDS Project
132 W. 43rd St.
New York, NY 10036
(212) 944-9800
fax: (212) 869-9065
Internet: http://www.aclu.org

The ACLU is the nation's oldest and largest civil liberties organization. Its Lesbian and Gay Rights/AIDS Project, started in 1986, handles litigation, education, and public-policy work on behalf of gays and lesbians. The union supports same-sex marriage. It publishes the monthly newsletter *Civil Liberties Alert*, the handbook *The Rights of Lesbians and Gay Men*, the briefing paper "Lesbian and Gay Rights," and the book *The Rights of Families: The ACLU Guide to the Rights of Today's Family Members*.

Canadian Lesbian and Gay Archives
Box 639, Station A
Toronto, ON M5W 1G2
CANADA
(416) 777-2755
Internet: http://www.clga.ca/archives

The archives collects and maintains information and materials relating to the gay and lesbian rights movement in Canada and elsewhere. Its collection of records and other materials documenting the stories of lesbians and gay men and their organizations in Canada is available to the public for the purpose of education and research. It also publishes an annual newsletter, *Lesbian and Gay Archivist*.

Concerned Women for America (CWA)
370 L'Enfant Promenade SW, Suite 800
Washington, DC 20024
(202) 488-7000
fax: (202) 488-0806

The CWA is an educational and legal defense foundation that seeks to strengthen the traditional family by applying Judeo-Christian moral standards. It opposes gay marriage and the granting of additional civil rights pro-

116

tections to gays and lesbians. It publishes the monthly magazine *Family Voice* and various position papers on gay marriage and other issues.

Eagle Forum
PO Box 618
Alton, IL 62002
(618) 462-5415

A political action group, Eagle Forum advocates traditional, biblical values. It believes mothers should stay home with their children, and it favors policies that support the traditional family and reduce government involvement in family issues. The forum opposes an equal rights amendment and gay rights legislation. It publishes the monthly *Phyllis Schlafly Report* and the *Eagle Forum Newsletter*.

Equal Rights Marriage Fund (ERMF)
2001 M St. NW
Washington, DC 20036
(202) 822-6546
fax: (202) 466-3540

The ERMF is dedicated to the legalization of gay and lesbian marriage and serves as a national clearinghouse for information on same-sex marriage. The organization publishes several brochures and articles, including *Gay Marriage: A Civil Right*.

Family Research Council (FRC)
801 G St. NW
Washington, DC 20001
(202) 393-2100
fax: (202) 393-2134
Internet: http://www.frc.org

The council is a research and educational organization that promotes the traditional family, which the council defines as a group of people bound by marriage, blood, or adoption. The council opposes gay marriage and adoption rights. It publishes numerous reports from a conservative perspective on issues affecting the family, including "Free to Be Family." Among its other publications are the monthly newsletter *Washington Watch* and the bimonthly journal *Family Policy*.

Family Research Institute (FRI)
PO Box 62640
Colorado Springs, CO 80962
(303) 681-3113

The FRI distributes information about family, sexual, and substance abuse issues. The institute believes that strengthening marriage would reduce many social problems, including crime, poverty, and sexually transmitted diseases. The FRI publishes the bimonthly newsletter *Family Research Report* as well as the position paper "What's Wrong with Gay Marriage?"

Focus on the Family
8605 Explorer Dr.
Colorado Springs, CO 80920
(719) 531-3400

Focus on the Family is a Christian organization that seeks to strengthen the traditional family in America. It believes the family is the most important social unit and maintains that reestablishing the traditional two-parent family will end many social problems. In addition to conducting research and educational programs, Focus on the Family publishes the monthly periodical *Focus on the Family* and the reports "Setting the Record Straight: What Research *Really* Says About the Consequences of Homosexuality" and "Twice As Strong: The Undeniable Advantages of Raising Children in a Traditional Two-Parent Family."

IntiNet Resource Center
PO Box 4322
San Rafael, CA 94913
e-mail: pad@well.com

The center promotes nonmonogamous relationships as an alternative to the traditional family. It also serves as a clearinghouse for information on nonmonogamous relationships and as a network for people interested in alternative family lifestyles. IntiNet publishes the quarterly newsletter *Floodtide,* the book *Polyamory: The New Love Without Limits,* and the *Resource Guide for the Responsible Non-Monogamist.*

Lambda Legal Defense Fund
666 Broadway, Suite 1200
New York, NY 10012-2317
(212) 995-8585
fax: (212) 995-2306

Lambda is a public interest law firm committed to achieving full recognition of the civil rights of lesbians, gay men, and people with HIV/AIDS. The firm addresses a variety of topics, including equal marriage rights, parenting and relationship issues, and domestic-partner benefits. It believes marriage is a basic right and an individual choice. Lambda publishes the quarterly *Lambda Update,* the pamphlet *Freedom to Marry,* and several position papers on same-sex marriage.

Lesbian Mothers National Defense Fund (LMNDF)
PO Box 21567
Seattle, WA 98111
(206) 325-2643

The LMNDF is a volunteer resource network that provides information, referrals, and emotional support to lesbians concerned with issues of child custody and visitation, artificial insemination, and adoption. It publishes the quarterly newsletter *Mom's Apple Pie* and a bibliography of materials concerning lesbian mothers.

Loving More
PO Box 4358
Boulder, CO 80306
(303) 534-7540
e-mail: ryan@lovemore.com
Internet: http://www.lovemore.com

Loving More explores and supports many different forms of family and relationships. It promotes alternative relationship options—such as open marriage, extended family, and multipartner marriages—and serves as a national clearinghouse for the multipartner movement. The organization publishes the quarterly magazine *Loving More.*

National Center for Lesbian Rights
870 Market St., Suite 570
San Francisco, CA 94102
(415) 392-8442

The center is a public interest law office that provides legal counseling and representation to victims of sexual-orientation discrimination. Primary areas of advice include child custody and parenting, employment, housing, the military, and insurance. Among the center's publications are the handbooks *Recognizing Lesbian and Gay Families: Strategies for Obtaining Domestic Partners Benefits* and *Lesbian and Gay Parenting: A Psychological and Legal Perspective.*

National Gay and Lesbian Task Force (NGLTF)
2320 17th St. NW
Washington, DC 20009-2702
(202) 332-6483
fax: (202) 332-0207

The NGLTF is a civil rights advocacy organization that lobbies Congress and the White House on a range of civil rights and AIDS issues affecting gays and lesbians. The organization is working to make same-sex marriage legal. It publishes numerous papers and pamphlets, the booklet *To Have and to Hold: Organizing for Our Right to Marry,* the fact sheet "Lesbian and Gay Families," the quarterly *NGLTF Newsletter,* and the monthly *Activist Alert.*

Parents and Friends of Lesbians and Gays (P-FLAG)
PO Box 27605
Washington, DC 20038-7605
(800) 432-6459

P-FLAG is a national organization that provides support and education services for gays, lesbians, bisexuals, and their families and friends. It also works to end prejudice and discrimination against homosexuals. It publishes and distributes pamphlets and articles, including *Why Is My Child Gay?, About Our Children,* and *Coming Out to My Parents.*

The Rockford Institute
Center on the Family in America
934 N. Main St.
Rockford, IL 61103
(815) 964-5811
fax: (815) 965-1826

The Rockford Institute works to return America to Judeo-Christian values and supports traditional roles for men and women. Its Center on the Family in America studies the evolution of the family and the effects of divorce on society. The institute publishes *Family in America* and *Chronicles,* both of which are monthly periodicals, and the newsletter *Main Street Memorandum.*

Traditional Values Coalition
139 C St. SE
Washington, DC 20003
(202) 547-8570
fax: (202) 546-6403

The coalition strives to restore what the group believes are the traditional moral and spiritual values in American government, schools, media, and society. It believes that gay marriage threatens the family unit and extends civil rights beyond what the coalition considers appropriate limits. The coalition publishes the quarterly newsletter *Traditional Values Report* as well as various information papers addressing same-sex marriage and other issues.

**The Universal Fellowship of Metropolitan Community Churches
(UFMCC)**
5300 Santa Monica Blvd., Suite 304
Los Angeles, CA 90029
(213) 464-5100

The UFMCC supports the lesbian and gay community with three hundred churches in sixteen countries. It publishes a wide range of materials on topics concerning religion and homosexuality, including *Not a Sin, Not a Sickness* and *Homosexuality and the Conservative Christian.*

Bibliography

Books

Henry J. Aaron, Thomas E. Mann, and Timothy Taylor, eds.	*Values and Public Policy*. Washington, DC: Brookings Institution, 1994.
Robert M. Baird and M. Katherine Baird, eds.	*Homosexuality: Debating the Issues*. Amherst, NY: Prometheus Books, 1995.
Robert M. Baird and Stuart E. Rosenbaum, eds.	*Same-Sex Marriage: The Moral and Legal Debate*. Amherst, NY: Prometheus Books, 1997.
Bruce Bawer, ed.	*Beyond Queer: Challenging Gay Left Orthodoxy*. New York: Free Press, 1996.
John Boswell	*Same-Sex Unions in Premodern Europe*. New York: Villard, 1994.
Reuven P. Bulka	*One Man, One Woman, One Lifetime: An Argument for Moral Tradition*. Lafayette, LA: Huntington House, 1995.
Robert P. Cabaj and David W. Purcell	*Same-Sex Marriage: A Supportive Guide to Psychological, Political, and Legal Issues*. San Francisco: Jossey-Bass, 1997.
Christopher Clulow, ed.	*Women, Men, and Marriage*. Northvale, NJ: Aaronson, 1996.
D. Merilee Clunis and G. Dorsey Green	*The Lesbian Parenting Book: A Guide to Creating Families and Raising Children*. Seattle, WA: Seal Press, 1995.
William N. Eskridge Jr.	*The Case for Same-Sex Marriage: From Sexual Liberty to Civilized Commitment*. New York: Free Press, 1996.
David M. Estlund and Martha Craven Nussbaum, eds.	*Sex, Preference, and Family: Essays on Laws and Nature*. New York: Oxford University Press, 1996.
George Grant and Mark A. Horne	*Legislating Immorality: The Homosexual Movement Comes Out of the Closet*. Franklin, TN: Moody Press and Legacy Communications, 1993.
Michael Nava and Robert Dawidoff	*Created Equal: Why Gay Rights Matter to America*. New York: St. Martin's Press, 1994.
David Popenoe	*Life Without Father: Compelling New Evidence That Fatherhood and Marriage Are Indispensable for the Good of Children and Society*. New York: Martin Kessler, 1996.
David Popenoe, Jean Bethke Elshtain, and David Blankenhorn, eds.	*Promises to Keep: Decline and Renewal of Marriage in America*. Lanham, MD: Rowman & Littlefield, 1996.

Thomas E. Schmidt   *Straight and Narrow?: Compassion and Clarity in the Homo-sexuality Debate.* Downers Grove, IL: Intervarsity Press, 1995.

Mark Philip Strasser   *Legally Wed: Same-Sex Marriage and the Constitution.* Ithaca, NY: Cornell University Press, 1997.

Andrew Sullivan   *Same-Sex Marriage: Pro and Con: A Reader.* New York: Vintage Books, 1997.

Andrew Sullivan   *Virtually Normal: An Argument About Homosexuality.* New York: Knopf, 1995.

Urvashi Vaid   *Virtual Equality: The Mainstreaming of Gay and Lesbian Liberation.* New York: Anchor Books, 1995.

Periodicals

K. Anthony Appiah   "The Marrying Kind," *New York Review of Books*, June 20, 1996.

Hadley Arkes   "A Culture Corrupted," *First Things*, November 1996. Available from PO Box 3000, Denville, NJ 07834.

Hadley Arkes   "Odd Couples," *National Review*, August 12, 1996.

Hadley Arkes   "Will Hawaii's Imperial Judges Give Us Gay Marriage in 1996?" *American Enterprise*, May/June 1995.

Bob Barr   "Would Legal Recognition of Same-Sex Marriage Be Good for America? No: Don't Let Homosexual Activity Subvert the Cornerstone of Civilized Society," *Insight*, June 10, 1996. Available from 3600 New York Ave. NE, Washington, DC 20002.

Walter Berns   "Marriage, Anyone?" *First Things*, April 1996.

Frank Browning   "Why Marry?" *New York Times*, April 17, 1996.

Mona Charen   "Marriage Isn't a Basic Human Right," *Conservative Chronicle*, July 17, 1996. Available from Box 29, Hampton, IA 50441.

Charles S. Clark   "National Campaign for Same-Sex Marriage Draws Political and Religious Opposition," *CQ Researcher*, May 10, 1996. Available from 1414 22nd St. NW, Washington, DC 20037.

Charles Colson and   "Why Not Gay Marriage?" *Christianity Today*, October
Nancy Pearcey   28, 1996.

Commonweal   "Marriage's True Ends," May 17, 1996.

David Orgon Coolidge   "The Dilemma of Same-Sex Marriage," *Crisis*, July/August 1996. Available from PO Box 10559, Riverton, NJ 08076-0559.

Dennis Cooper   "Altared State," *Spin*, March 1997. Available from 6 W. 18th St., New York, NY 10011-4608

Jonathan Curiel   "The Little City That Could," *Advocate*, March 13, 1997.

Anne-Marie Cusac	"Tying the Gordian Knot," *Progressive,* January 1997.
David W. Dunlap	"Some Gay Rights Advocates Question Effort to Defend Same-Sex Marriage," *New York Times,* June 7, 1996.
Economist	"Let Them Wed," January 6, 1996.
William N. Eskridge Jr.	"Would Legal Recognition of Same-Sex Marriage Be Good for America? Yes: Marriage Will Normalize Social Relations Between Gay and Straight People Throughout the Culture," *Insight,* June 10, 1996.
Barbara Findlen	"Is Marriage the Answer?" *Ms.,* May/June 1995.
John Gallagher	"Marriage Compromised," *Advocate,* May 27, 1997.
Michelle Garcia	"Altared States: Same Sex Marriage and Civil Rights," *Third Force,* March/April 1996.
Richard Goldstein	"It Ain't Over Till It's Over," *Village Voice,* August 13, 1996. Available from 36 Cooper Sq., New York, NY 10003.
E.J. Graff	"Retying the Knot," *Nation,* June 24, 1996.
Thomas W. Hazlett	"For Better or Worse," *Reason,* July 1996.
Katia Hetter	"The New Civil Rights Battle," *U.S. News & World Report,* June 3, 1996.
Issues and Controversies on File	"Same-Sex Marriage," April 19, 1996. Available from Facts On File News Services, 11 Penn Plaza, New York, NY 10001-2006.
Fenton Johnson	"Wedded to an Illusion," *Harper's,* November 1996.
David A. Kaplan and Daniel Klaidman	"A Battle, Not the War," *Newsweek,* June 3, 1996.
Ken I. Kersch	"Full Faith and Credit for Same-Sex Marriages?" *Political Science Quarterly,* Spring 1997.
Melanie Kirkpatrick	"Gay Marriage: Who Should Decide?" *Wall Street Journal,* March 13, 1996.
Robert H. Knight	"Mom-and-Dad Homes Help Mold Healthy Kids," *Insight,* July 25, 1994.
Andrew Koppelman	"No Fantasy Island," *New Republic,* August 7, 1995.
Charles Krauthammer	"When John and Jim Say, 'I Do,'" *Time,* July 22, 1996.
James Kunen	"Hawaiian Courtship," *Time,* December 16, 1996.
Kim A. Lawton	"State Lawmakers Scramble to Ban Same-Sex Marriages," *Christianity Today,* February 3, 1997.
David Mixner	"No One Has to Send a Gift," *Time,* December 16, 1996.
Katha Pollit	"Gay Marriage? Don't Say I Didn't Warn You," *Nation,* April 29, 1996.
Jonathan Rauch	"For Better or Worse?" *New Republic,* May 6, 1996.

Jonathan Rauch   "A Pro-Gay, Pro-Family Policy," *Wall Street Journal*, November 29, 1994.

Gabriel Rotello   "To Have and to Hold: The Case for Gay Marriage," *Nation*, June 24, 1996.

Lisa Schiffren   "Gay Marriage, an Oxymoron," *New York Times,* March 23, 1996.

Richard Stengel   "For Better or for Worse?" *Time*, June 3, 1996.

Andrew Sullivan   "Hawaiian Aye," *New Republic*, December 30, 1996.

Andrew Sullivan   "Three's a Crowd," *New Republic*, June 17, 1996.

Andrew Sullivan   "What You Do," *New Republic*, March 18, 1996.

Guinevere Turner   "'I, Melanie, Take You, Mary...,'" *Glamour,* February 1997.

U.S. News & World Report   "Should Gay Marriage Be Legal?" June 3, 1996.

James Q. Wilson   "Against Homosexual Marriage," *Commentary*, March 1996.

Index